Take Flight

Fun with Textile Collage

Emily Taylor

Dedicated to my husband, Joseph, who provides me with unwavering support.

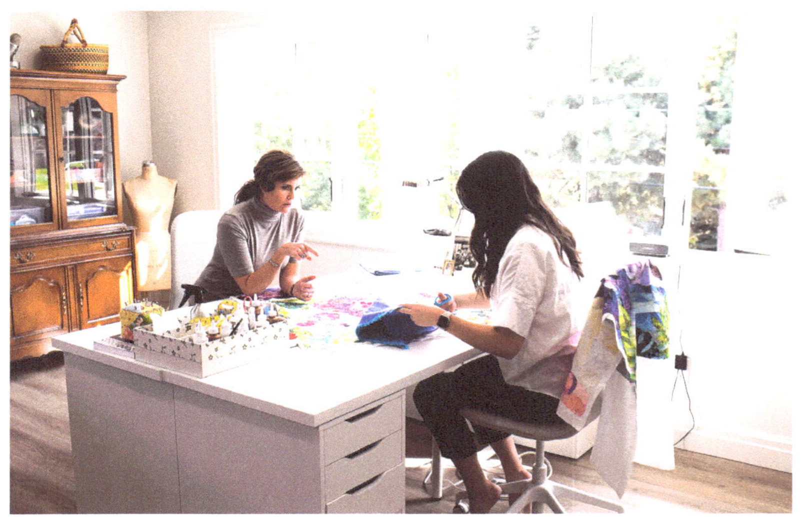

Acknowledgments

I'm grateful to Quinn Silcox, who has used her immense talent as a writer to edit this book, (and for being my best friend)!

A huge thank you to my adorable daughter, Amelia Whiting! She has photographed everything you see in this book and kept me laughing through it all.

TABLE OF CONTENTS

<u>Introduction</u>   4

<u>Chapter One • Understanding Theory</u>   7
  Color Families
  Value
  Temperature
  Contrast
  Impressionist Collage

<u>Chapter Two • Supplies for Textile Collage</u> 14
  Fabric
  Fusible Web
  Scissors
  Parchment Paper
  Work Surface
  Irons & Pressing Mat
  Design Template

<u>Chapter Three • Making the Birds</u>   23
  Select Fabric
  Prepare Fabric
  Apply Fabric: Parchment Pressing

<u>Chapter Four • Creating a Composition</u>   49
  Harmony
  Balance
  Scale

<u>Chapter Five • Projects</u>   53
  Art Quilt
  Embroidered Wall Art
  Decorative Pillow

<u>Artist's Gallery</u>   72

<u>Appendix</u>   81

<u>About the Author</u>   89

<u>Additional Resources</u>   90

INTRODUCTION

Hello! I'm glad to have you join me on this exploration into creating birds with fabric! I'd like to share a bit more about who I am and what led to our "paths crossing" through this book. I'm Emily Taylor, creative entrepreneur, designer and collage quilt artist.

My journey into the world of textiles began as an effort to preserve my sanity when I was a young mom, home with my children all day. Don't get me wrong, I love being a mother, but I'm a creative, ambitious person and I needed more in my life besides diapers, cooking and play-dates. I wanted to do something from home so I could still focus on my primary role as a mom. I landed upon the idea that I would like to design quilt fabric (I was a mural artist prior to having children). The only catch was that I first had to develop the skills to create digital artwork, something I never even knew was possible. I bought a computer and design software, and set about teaching myself how to use them. During that period, I would put my kids to bed each night and head to my room for hours of late-night learning. When I had developed just the basic skill set needed to submit a portfolio of design work, I was rewarded with a contract to design

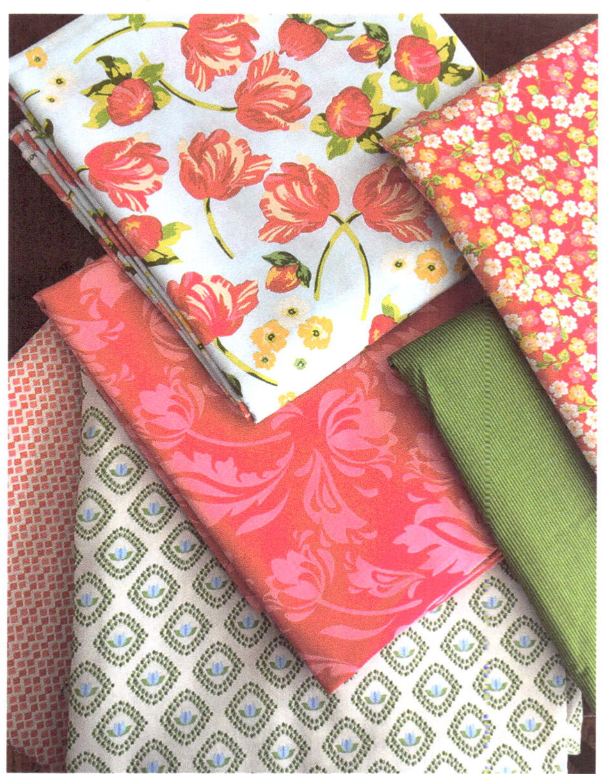

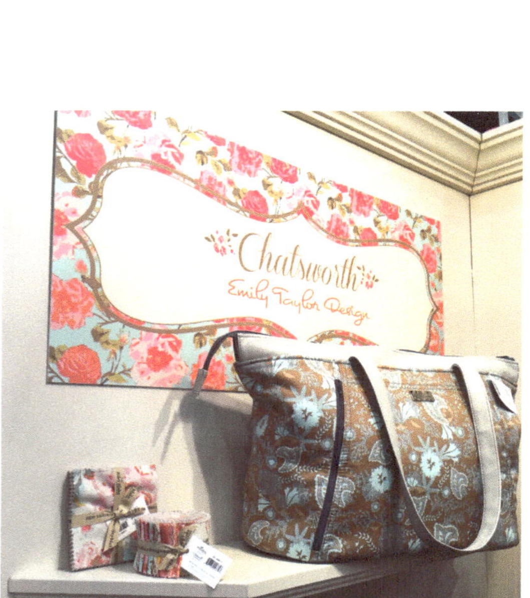

fabric with a major manufacturer. After creating more than a dozen fabric collections for this particular company (who shall remain nameless), I decided to concurrently launch a company called PatternJam. PatternJam was an amazing online tool that allowed users to create a quilt pattern, upload their own fabric and see what the finished quilt would look like. It also provided fabric requirements and cutting instructions for the user-created pattern.

Finally, PatternJam gave users the tools to create customized quilt tops, which were printed and shipped to the user. It was a great little company, but it was a threat to my relationship with the fabric company. Unfortunately, I was "relieved" of my status as one of their designers.

Additionally during this time I had partnered with an investor who had a vision for PatternJam that did not square with my own. The relationship soured (I was pushed out of the business entirely) and the company I had created was decimated. Everything I'd built up to that point was in ruins. The loss of PatternJam was extremely painful. However, from this difficult experience, I learned how to run a business (and how not to). It also challenged my resiliency and re-awakened my creativity. Sometimes, from the ashes of our most devastating failure comes the greatest success and clarity of purpose.

I decided at that time that I'd like to mold myself into the artist that I've always aspired to be.

I just didn't have the courage to go for it until the "rug was pulled out from under me". Why had it been so darn scary to pursue being an artist previously? I suppose because our nature is to avoid the pain of failure. But, having been through failure on a scale I didn't think I'd ever recover from, I realized that failure is not something to fear. Failure is a tool for growth. The only failure is not to try. So here I am. And here you are! Since you're reading this, you're probably on your own journey to be a better textile collage artist.

Today, I feel incredibly blessed that I was able to learn from the unfortunate end of PatternJam. Shortly following that episode I began to explore and experiment with collage quilts. I completed my first collage quilt in late 2017. My method for creating collage quilts is to apply traditional principles of art such as color theory, balance, and composition.

I continue to push myself in the developmental process and artistry of collage quilting. This pursuit has fulfilled my creative passions and has brought me joy! I hope to share that with you, my friends.

This book is a journal of my journey as a collage quilt artist and the lessons I've learned about how to be better. I learn best through making mistakes (failing). Hopefully after reading this book, you'll avoid some of the mistakes I've made along my journey. Becoming better at something requires growth. Growth requires discomfort. Let's get out of our comfort zones and create something amazing! That's what makers & creators do.

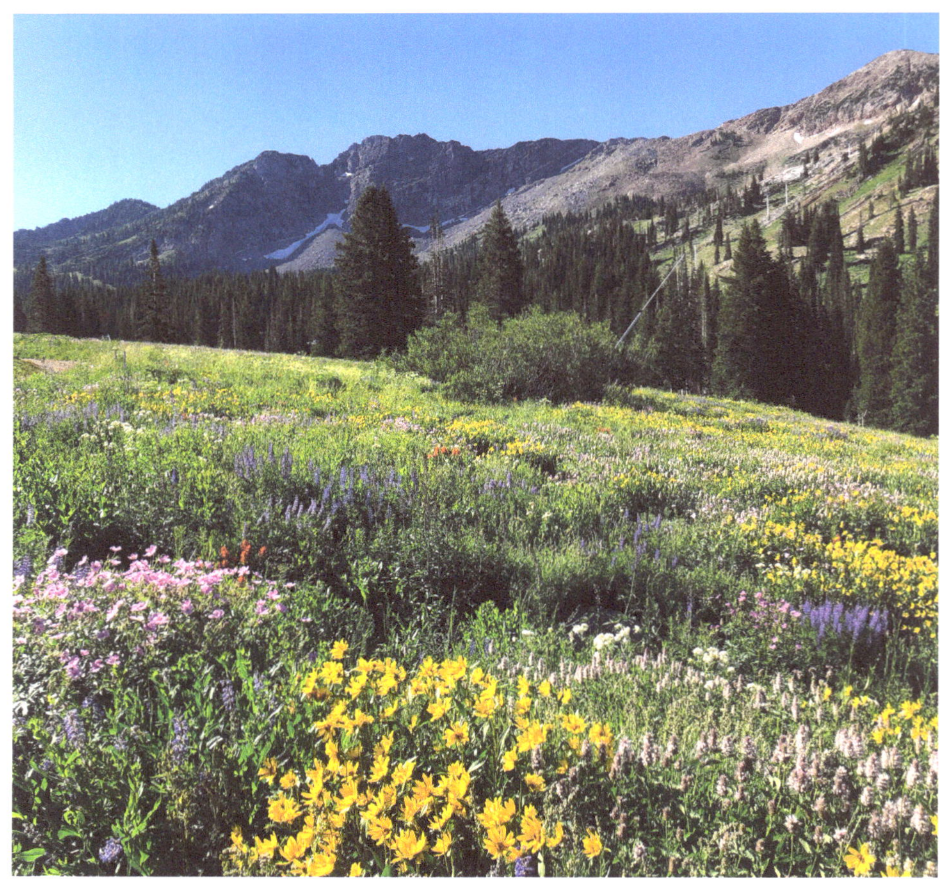

The projects in this book are inspired by my love of the outdoors. I'm a hiker, a mountain biker, and a skier. I'm overwhelmed at the stunning beauty of where I live at the base of the Wasatch mountain range in Sandy, Utah. One of my great pleasures when I'm outside is to observe the variety of birds in the foothills and mountains near my home.

I hope that each bird you choose to create from this book delivers the sense of calm and wonder that can be felt in nature. I hope that this book inspires you to appreciate the journey.

~Emily

It's important to understand some basic principles of color theory as we begin our journey in textile collage. We will apply these foundational principles to the selection of our fabric, as well as the execution of our projects, so pay attention! ;)

COLOR FAMILIES

The color wheel is comprised of a few different types of families that are important to keep in mind:

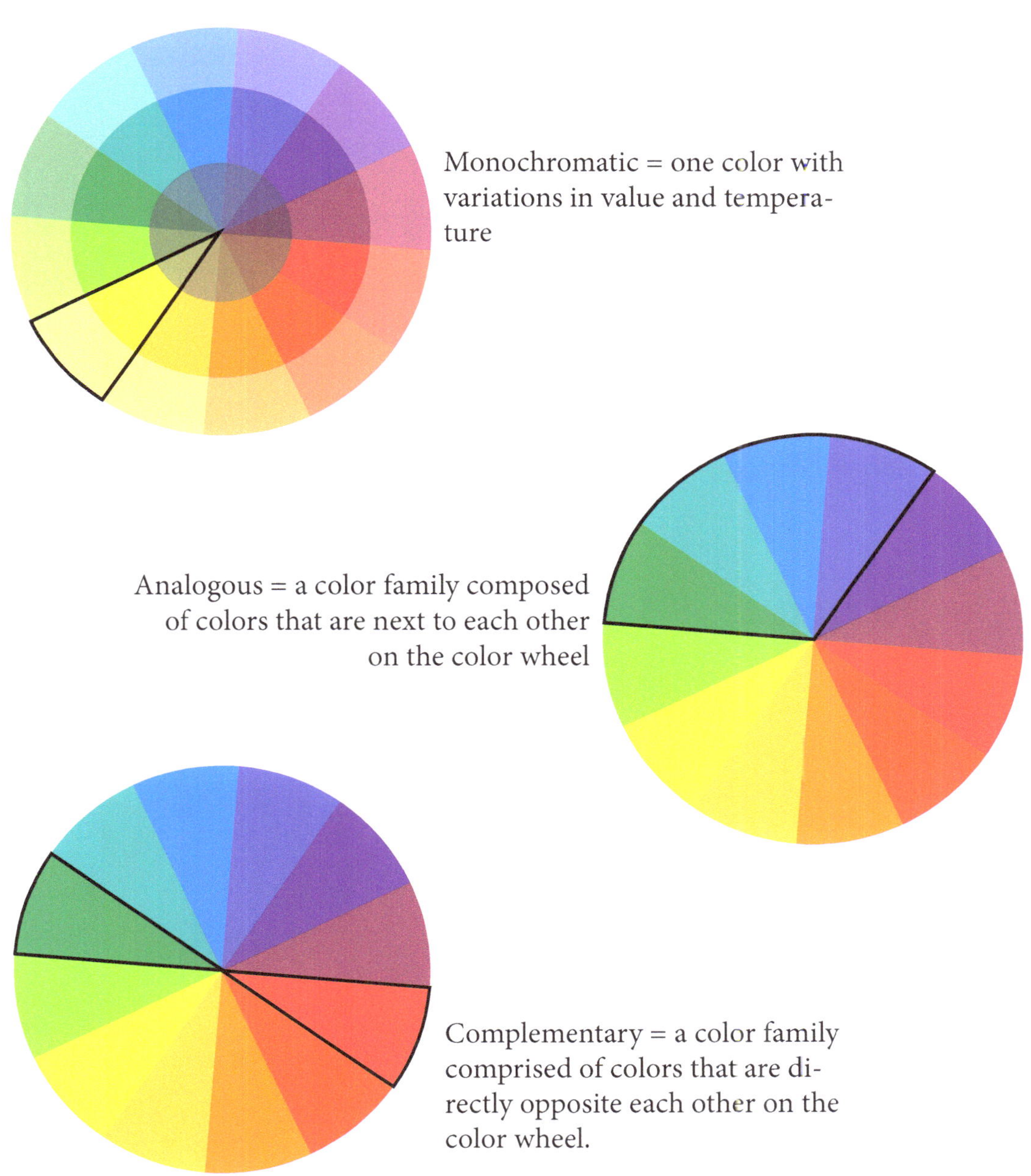

Monochromatic = one color with variations in value and temperature

Analogous = a color family composed of colors that are next to each other on the color wheel

Complementary = a color family comprised of colors that are directly opposite each other on the color wheel.

VALUE

For our purposes, value will refer to the lightness or darkness of a fabric. Every color in the spectrum can appear as light or dark or somewhere in between.

We can determine the value of a particular piece of fabric by comparing it with another piece of fabric of the same color-- this reveals the *RELATIVE VALUE* of each fabric. Through this simple method of comparing fabrics, we can determine whether the value of the two fabrics is similar, or if one is lighter or darker than the other. Easy-peasy!

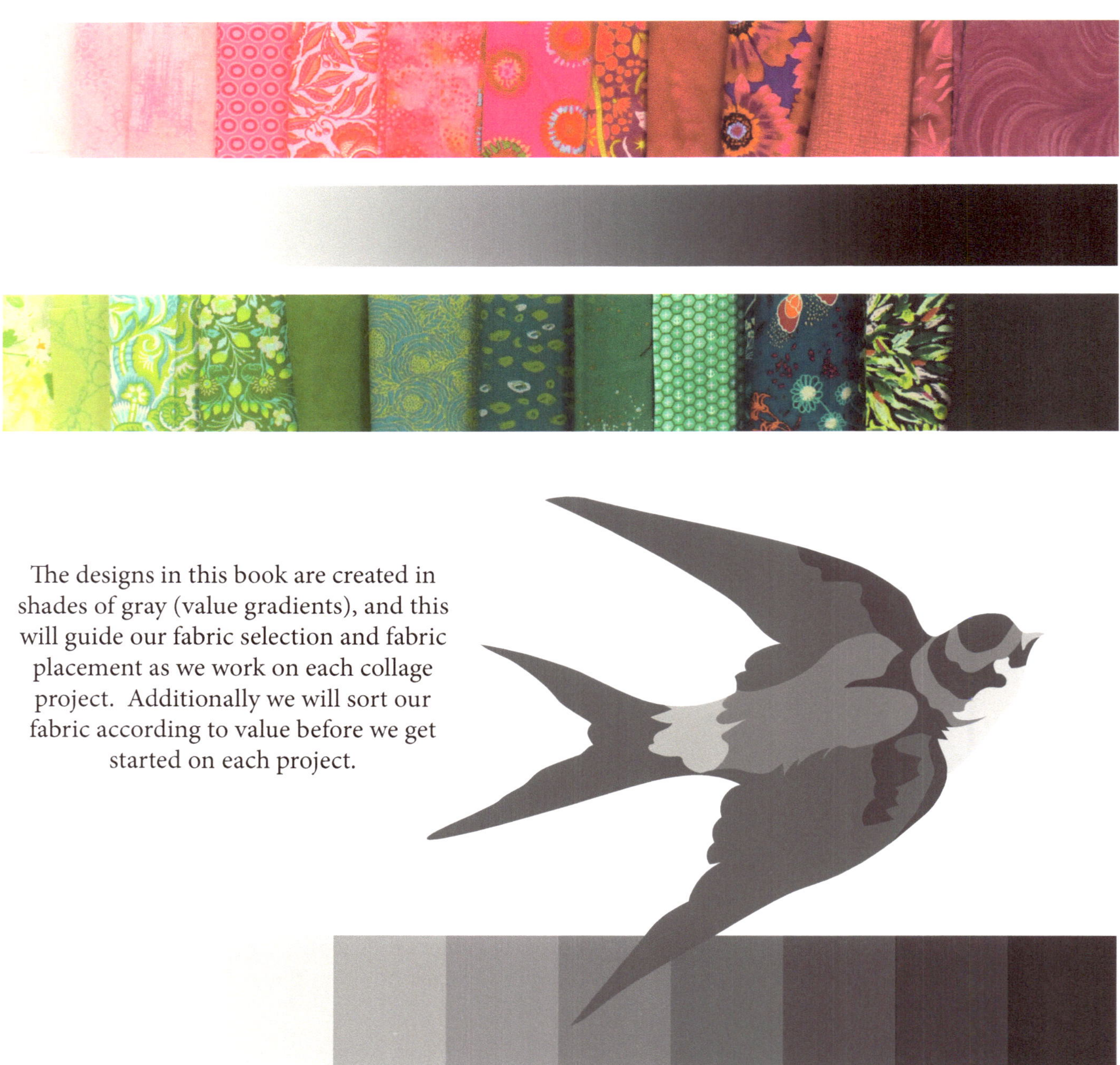

The designs in this book are created in shades of gray (value gradients), and this will guide our fabric selection and fabric placement as we work on each collage project. Additionally we will sort our fabric according to value before we get started on each project.

In addition to every color falling somewhere on the value spectrum, each color will also fall somewhere on the temperature spectrum between warm and cool. Yes, I know... you are thinking that only certain colors are warm and certain colors are cool. In a broad sense, that is TRUE! Blues, purples and teal are cool colors. Red, orange and yellow colors are warm colors.

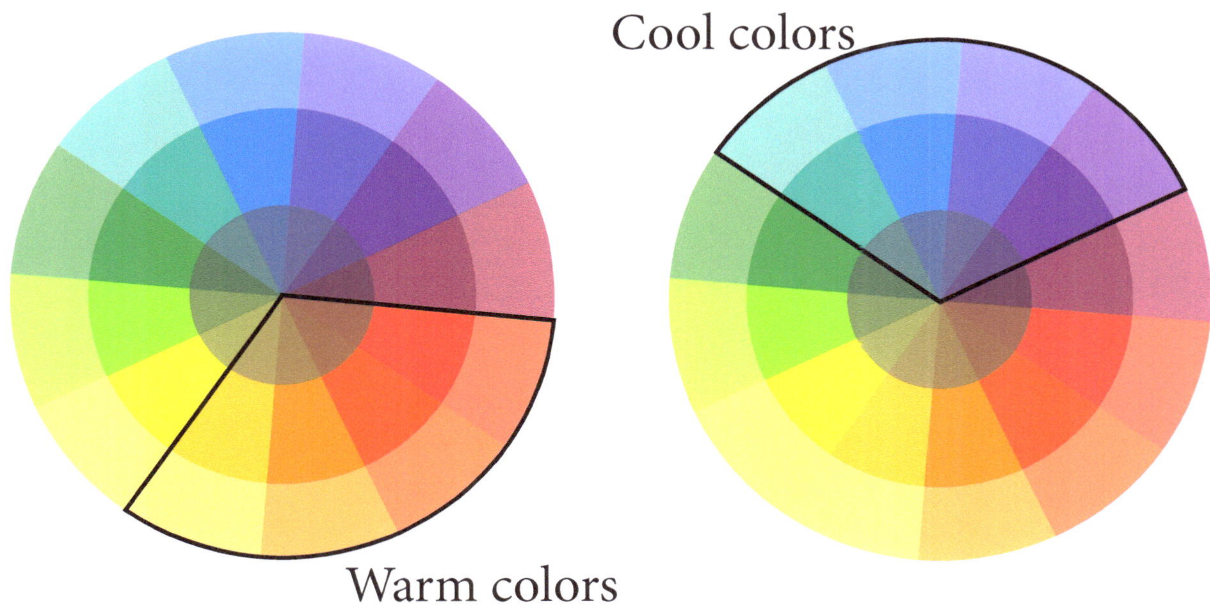

I find it helpful to also understand that as a color slides along the temperature spectrum, it will appear warmer or cooler depending on which direction it slides. For example, as green slides towards the cool end of the spectrum, it appears cooler-- these greens start to look teal. As it moves towards the warm end of the spectrum, it becomes warmer. Warm greens are described as yellow green and olive green.

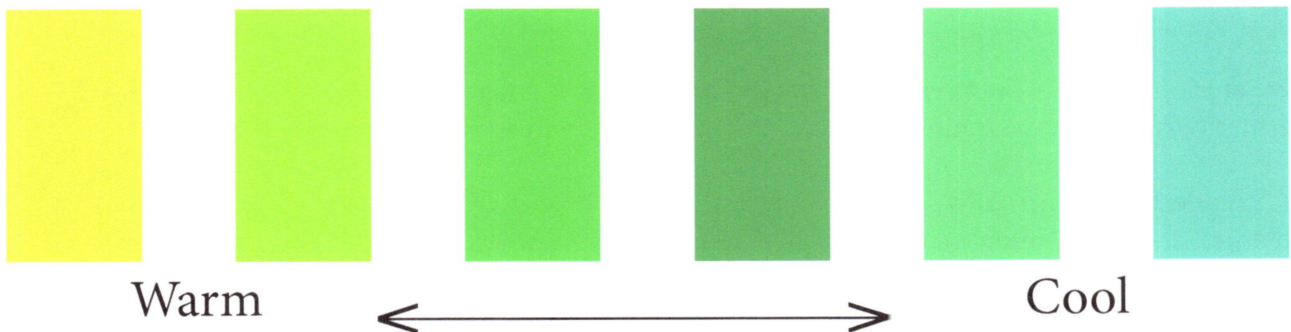

Every color will have warm and cool versions of itself depending on which direction they "slide" along the scale.

All colors in the spectrum can be expressed as warm or cool. Even colors like yellow, and red (very warm colors) can appear to have warmer or cooler versions. As with determining value, compare a piece of fabric with another piece of the same color to get a sense of the temperature.

RED

GREEN

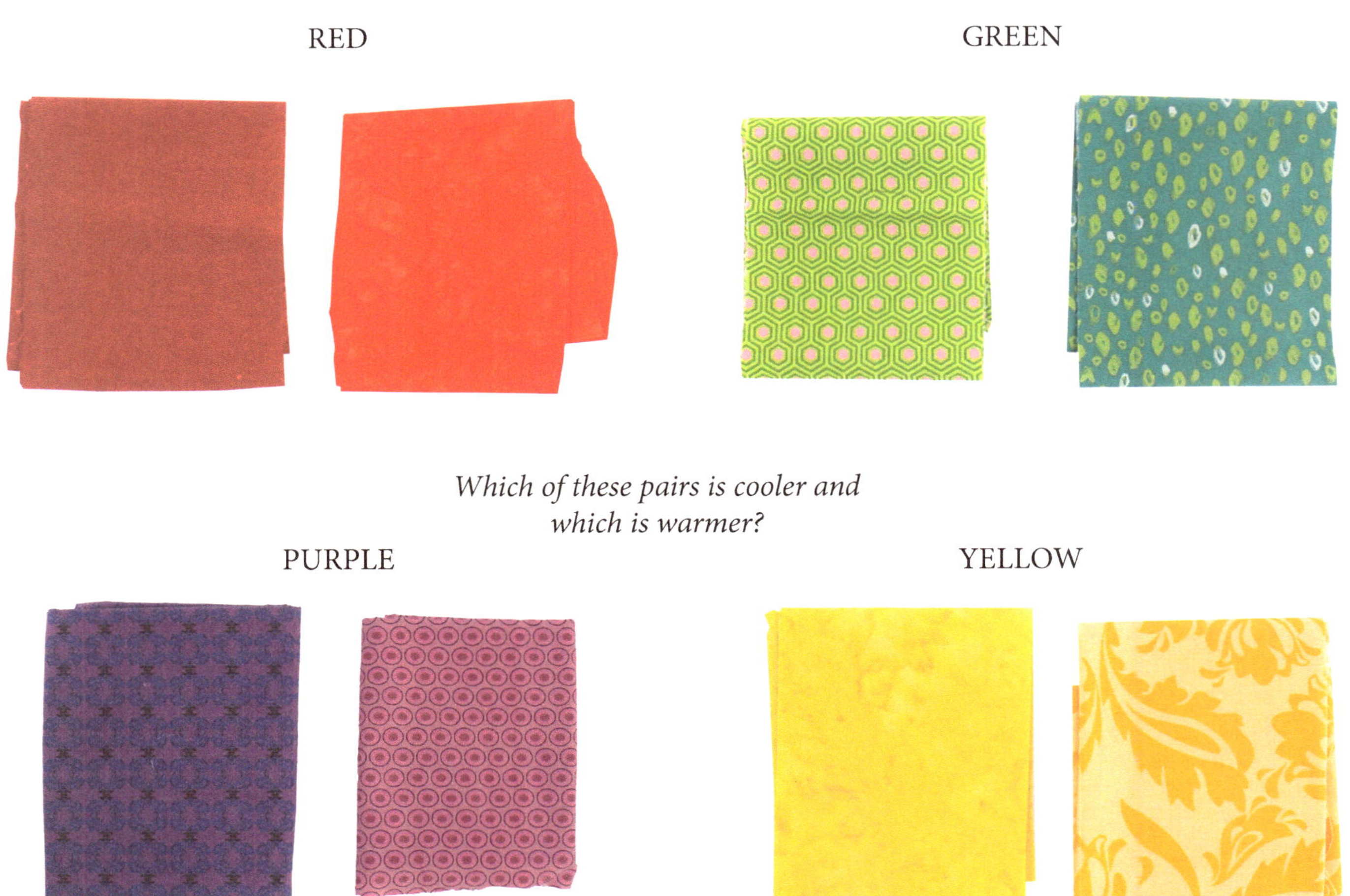

Which of these pairs is cooler and which is warmer?

PURPLE

YELLOW

Here are some *hints:* A warmer red will look more orange; A cooler green will appear more teal; A warmer purple will appear more maroon; A cooler yellow will seem to have more green in it.

In a composition, warm colors have the effect of coming forward. Warm colors grab the viewers attention, and can dominate a piece. Conversely, cool colors are calming and tend to recede in a composition. Because warm colors come forward and cool colors recede, placing warm and cool colors next to each other in a design creates a very subtle suggestion of movement. The object becomes more dynamic and alive!

Understanding this nuance about color helps us to create subtle contrast in our work.

The main reason that I bother with understanding the concepts of color, value, and temperature is because these are the tools that I use to create contrast. Contrast is the secret sauce when making a textile collage. It's what helps to define a design or motif so that we understand what we are looking at.

Contrast can be dramatic or subtle. Dramatic contrast is easily seen in complementary colors, or in the juxtaposition of light and dark fabric. Subtle contrast is achieved in the use of warm and cool versions of the same color next to each other, or in analogous color groupings.

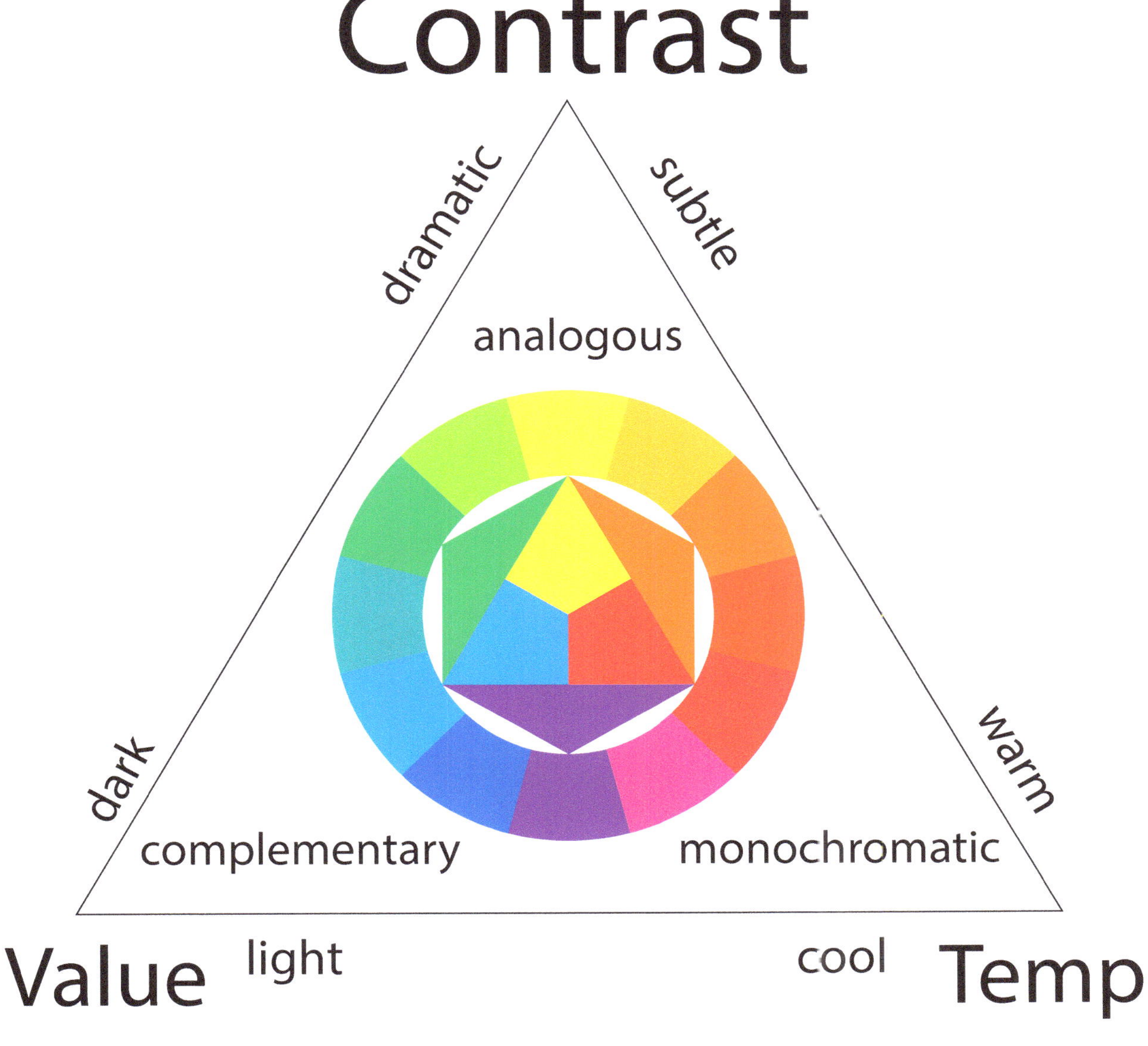

Refer to this chart as you select fabric and as you apply fabric to your collage. Awareness of these principles as we work with fabric in our textile collage projects will elevate the outcome of what we create, defining them as sophisticated works of art. And that is exactly what we want!

IMPRESSIONIST COLLAGE

I love the paintings of the Impressionist masters, Edgar Degas, Alfred Sisley, Camille Pissarro, and Claude Monet, among others. The artwork of the Impressionists represents a break from the traditional realism that was the standard for art up until that point in time. These artists promoted the idea that *suggestion*, rather than a pictorial representation could constitute art. They helped us to see that the interplay of light and dark, and of physical brushstrokes on a canvas can also become part of the artwork.

If you look at an impressionist painting up close, it can look like a jumbled mess of brushstrokes. It's only when you stand back from the painting, taking in the artwork as a whole does the piece become comprehensible and beautiful.

I liken the way I apply fabric pieces to a textile collage to Impressionism, because the individual shapes and sizes of each piece of fabric are quite haphazard.   Like an Impressionist painting, when you look at a collage quilt up close, it looks like a mess of fabric. But when you stand back to get the larger perspective, the individual fabric pieces disappear and the beauty of the entire composition becomes clear.

My method to create this impressionism is to use multiple pieces of fabric of the same value / color in each section of the design.

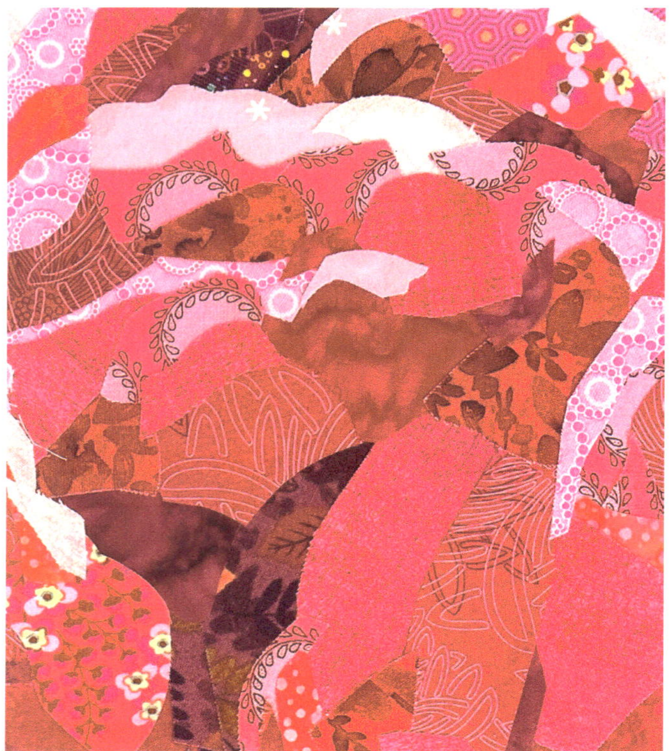
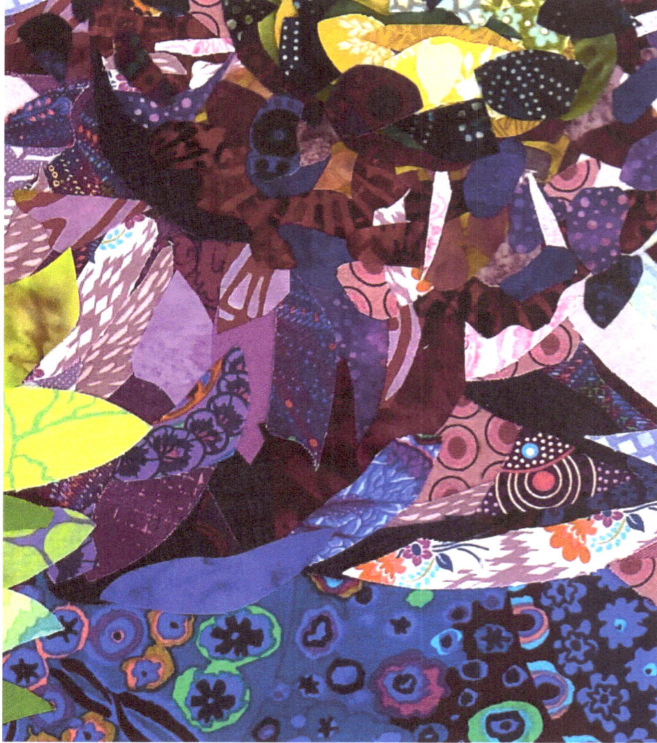

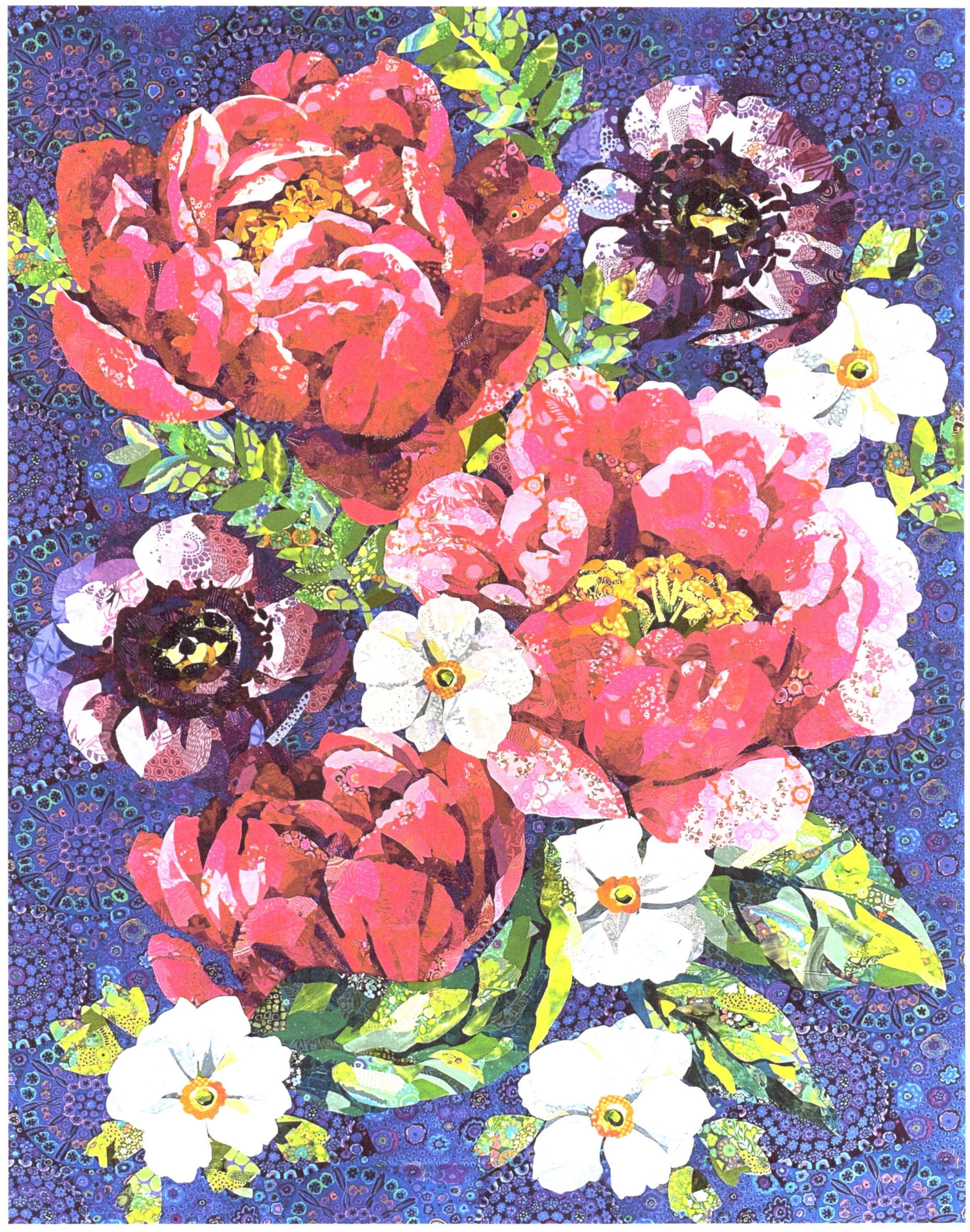

Chapter Two
Supplies for Textile Collage

FABRIC

The most important element in a successful textile collage project is a large variety of fabric! Here are my guidelines for selecting fabric and why I choose certain fabrics over others.

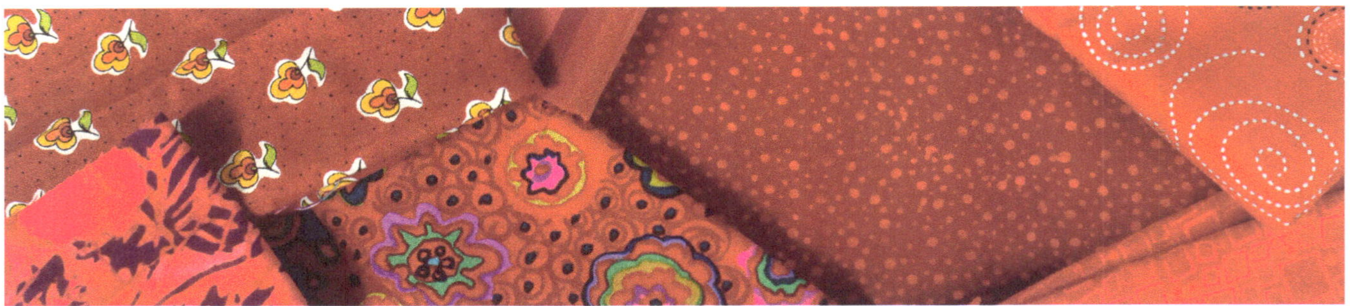

<u>Good Fabric for Textile Collage</u>

•*Batiks*. These beautiful fabrics are dyed rather than printed and tend to have a tighter weave than traditional quilting cotton. They come in a glorious spectrum of colors and values!   Most batiks have a clearly dominant color, but have movement and fluidity in a subtle design that solids don't have.

•*Designer fabrics*. There is a reason that quilt fabric designers have rock-star status in the quilt world: they know what they are doing with color, pattern, repeat and scale! Check out Tula Pink, Kaffe Fassett, Anna Maria Horner and Allison Glass, for starters. Furthermore, the quality of designer fabric is far above that of fabric found at discount stores like Walmart and Hobby Lobby. That's not to say you must use all designer fabric (which is expensive)-- a small amount is sufficient to bring that "special something" to your project.

•*Analogous colors*. There is something YUMMY about a fabric design that uses colors that are close to each other on the color wheel: fabric that mixes orange, red and pink; or teal, blue and purple. I LOVE to pull in analogous colors as I'm working on a collage project.

•*Fabric that mixes warm and cool* versions of the same color in the design. Oooo... yes! That subtle contrast brings a level of daring and sophistication to a textile collage and announces to the world that YOU know what you are doing with color!

•Designs that leave *little negative space*.

•*Fabric that you LOVE*. Even if fabric doesn't fall into the categories above, I often purchase fabric simply because I fall in love with it. It's these pieces that I turn to for inspiration about a color palette or that I will fussy-cut.

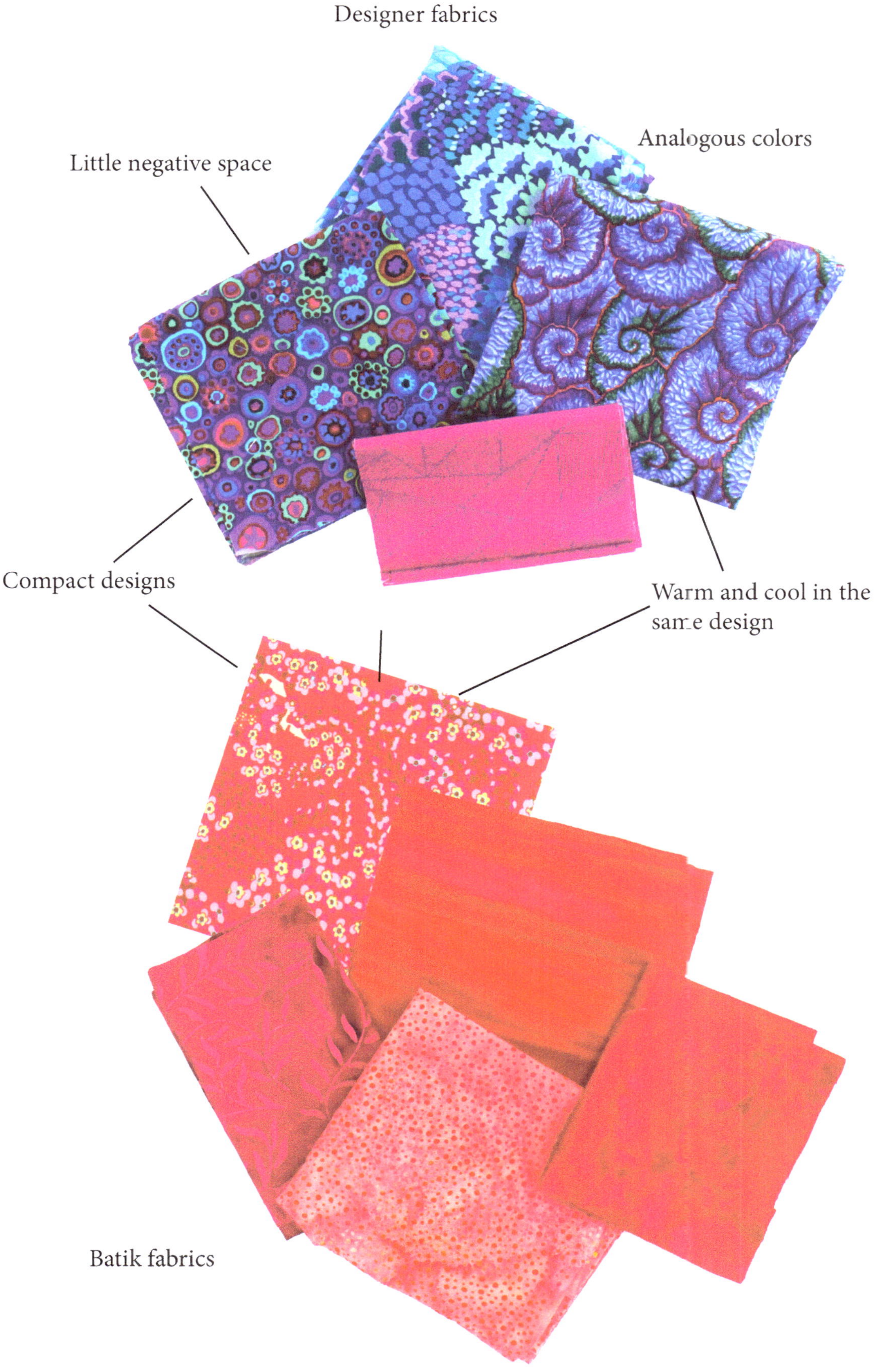

Designer fabrics
Analogous colors
Little negative space
Compact designs
Warm and cool in the same design
Batik fabrics

<u>F a b r i c   t o   u s e   SPARINGLY</u>

•**Solids**. I generally don't like to use solids in my collage projects. Solid fabrics tends to stand out too much when next to patterned fabric. The only solids that I like are woven cottons, but they fray more than traditional quilting cotton-- just something to keep in mind if you are averse to frayed edges.

•**Strong directional designs** like stripes and plaids. These types of fabrics don't play well with other fabrics because they tend to grab all the attention of a collage.

•**Polka dots**. Particularly large dots and if the repeat is a strong grid pattern. Random, small, scatter dots are alright.

•**High-contrast designs**. If you look at a piece of fabric and can't quickly determine the main color, it's probably because it has multiple colors competing for dominance. Similarly, design motifs that use complementary colors (orange / blue; green / red; yellow / purple) are high-contrast. Be careful about using them. If it's difficult to determine whether the fabric is mostly light or dark, you are looking at a high-contrast fabric design. Not my fave.

•Any design that uses **white with color**. When working on a section that is a mid-tone value, white will stick out like a sore thumb. This type of pattern is high-contrast.

•Fabric designs that uses **black with a color**. Ick. I just don't care for black. Like designs that use white, black creates too much contrast when used with mid-tone colors. Using black in a design is like a writer using swear words to express herself because she has a limited vocabulary. It's just so unimaginative.

•**Novelty fabric** that uses complex images or has strong motifs. Think: western landscape fabric that has digitally printed buffalo; or a pizza slice design with pepperoni polka dots. These types of fabric are generally NOT what I collect for my textile collage stash.

•**Sparse repeat**. Remember that I'm not a fan of solids, so if a design has a pattern that only repeats every 3" - 5" inches, it's going to have a large amount of solid color in the negative space.

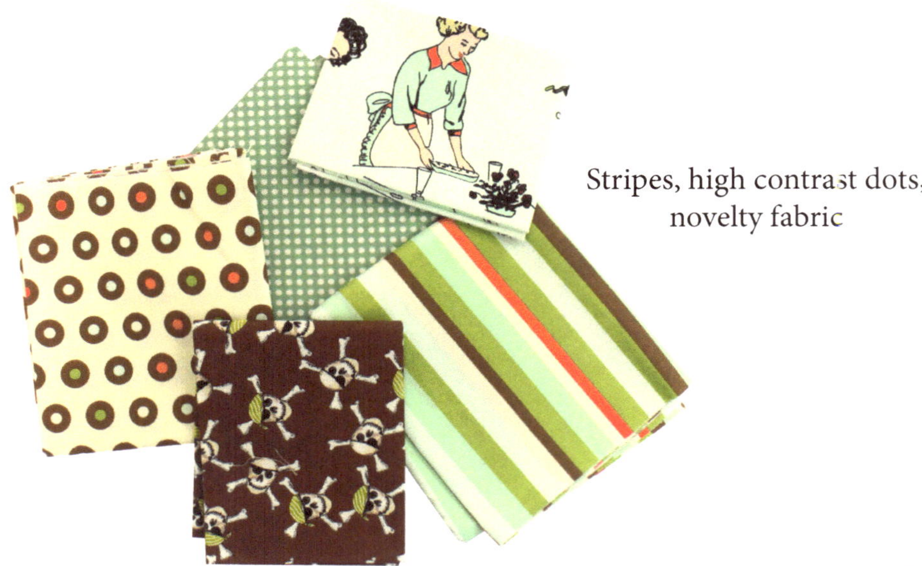

Stripes, high contrast dots, novelty fabric

Understanding and applying the basic principles of color theory will help to elevate the fabric choices for a textile collage and result in a more sophisticated design.

When I'm selecting fabric I begin by pulling all the fabric pieces that I think I might want to incorporate into my project, first by color. After I've selected the colors that I want to use in my project, I sort each color in a gradient from light to dark.

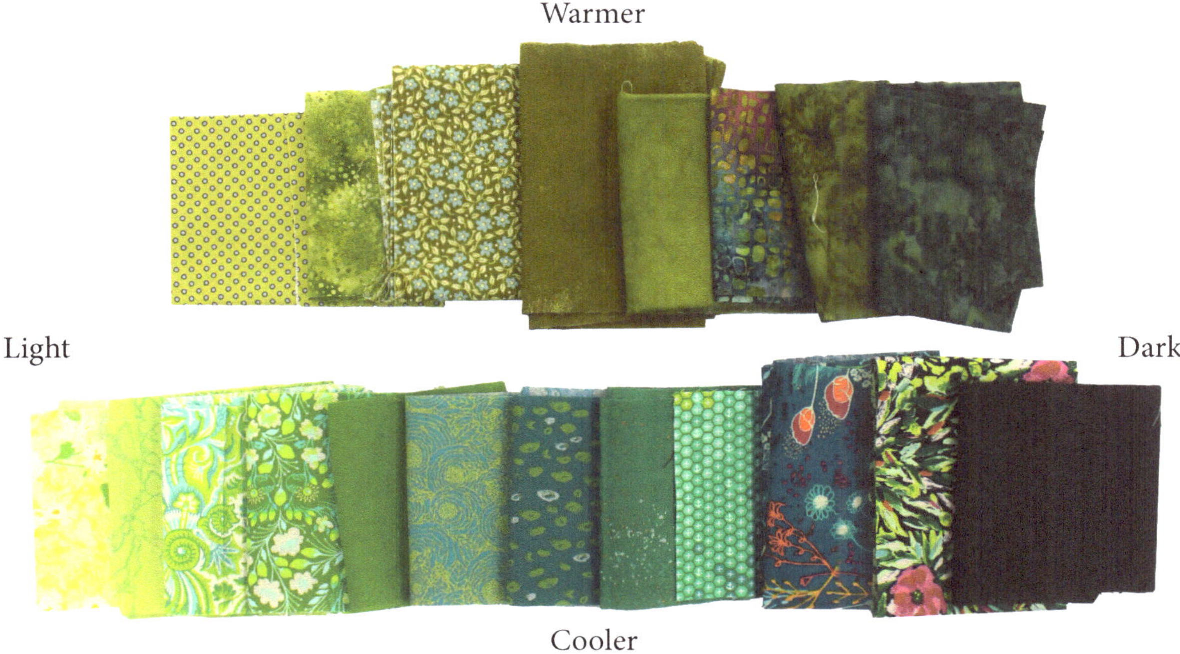

I make sure to include warm and cool variations of each color. Remember~ when a warm fabric is next to a cool fabric of the same color, the result is to create subtle movement and richness in the composition. It makes the collage look dimensional and artistic, and helps to avoid the flat look of an amateur piece.

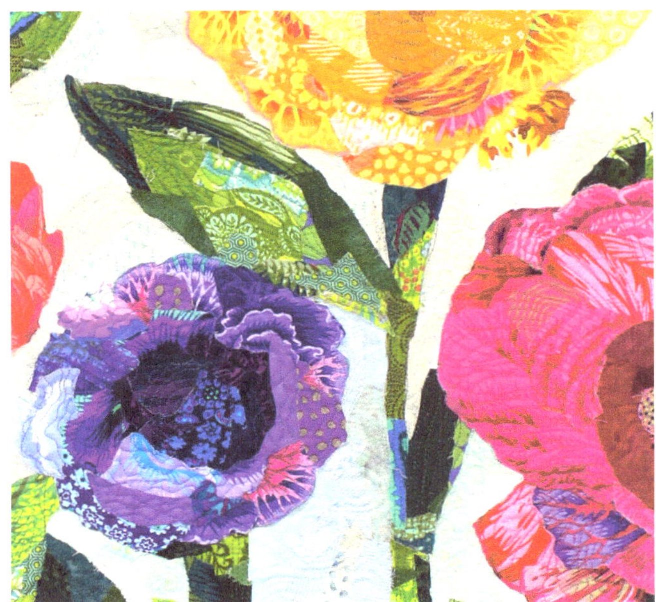

The leaves and stems in this design illustrate the effect of having warm and cool greens next to each other. The cool, darker greens juxtaposed with the bright yellow-green fabrics suggest that dappled sunlight is hitting the stem it and casting shadows underneath the flowers.

The amount of fabric required for a textile collage project is very fluid! Instead of offering specific guide-lines for the amount of fabric required, I always err on the side of "MORE". When I need to add to my stash of fabric, I generally don't purchase more than 1/8 of a yard of fabric. The only time I will purchase as much as a fat quarter is when the motif is large and it's something I might want to *FUSSY-CUT*.

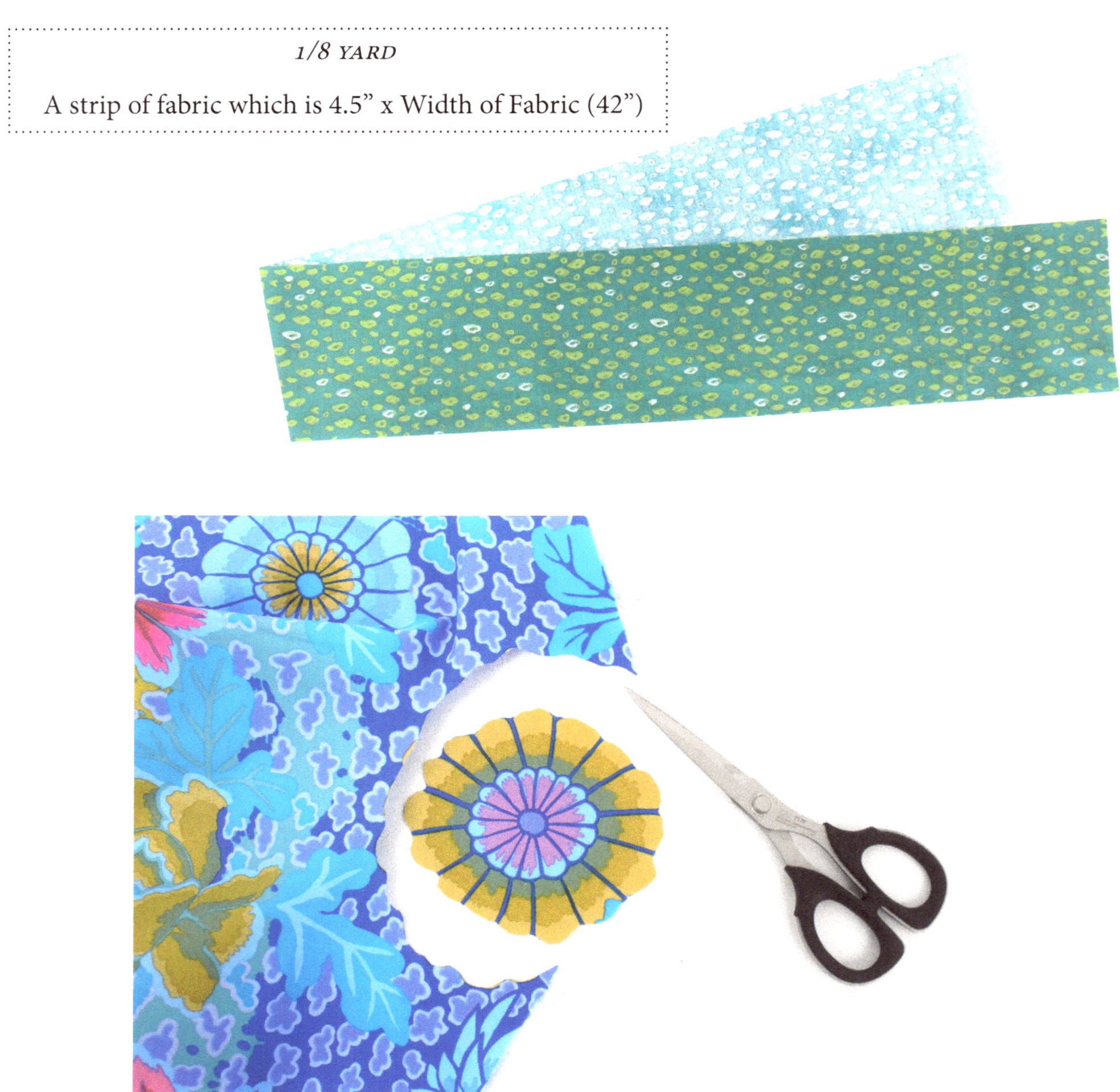

1/8 YARD

A strip of fabric which is 4.5" x Width of Fabric (42")

FUSSY-CUT

Cutting around a precise element
in the design of a piece of fabric

Textile collage requires an adhesive to fix each piece of fabric to the other pieces and to a foundation or background fabric. The adhesive used in the projects in this book is a double sided fusible web called Lite Steam a Seam 2* (SAS). While there are many options for adhesive, this product has become my favorite.

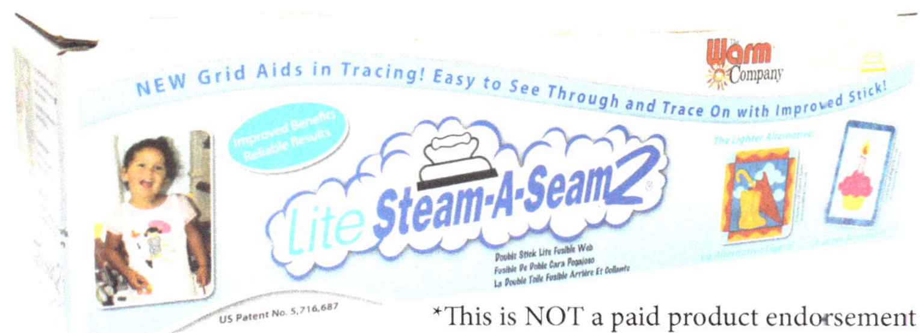

*This is NOT a paid product endorsement

<u>The Benefits of Using Lite Steam a Seam 2</u>

•There is a temporary layer of adhesive which allows me to replace a piece of fabric if I'm not happy with it prior to the final pressing
•It is easy to work with when using my "Parchment Pressing" method
•It provides a permanent adhesion once the piece is steamed and pressed
•There is a minimal amount of fraying on the edges of each piece of fabric because the adhesive is uniform across the back side of each piece

____

This is baking paper that can be purchased in the grocery store! Parchment paper is designed to be non-stick and to withstand heat, which makes it perfect for use in creating textile collage. The other advantages are that it is very inexpensive, it comes in a long roll, is semi-transparent and is reusable up to 3 times.

Parchment paper is essential when using the "Parchment Pressing" method. Because a collaged design will not permanently adhere to the parchment paper, I can create each design independently before adhering them permanently to the background fabric. Each collaged piece can be peeled off the parchment paper in one piece- like a sticker!

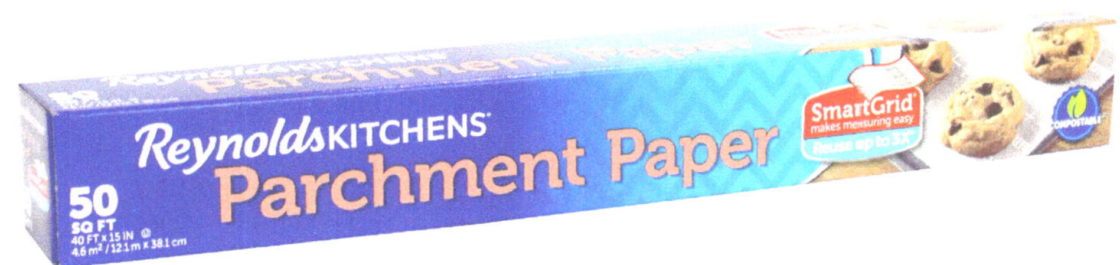

SCISSORS

The scissors that I prefer are those that have a tiny serrated edge, so that they cut fabric pieces efficiently without slipping, as can happen with smooth blades. I also prefer to work with a size that corresponds to the size of cuts that I make. This means scissors in the range of 6" is perfect.

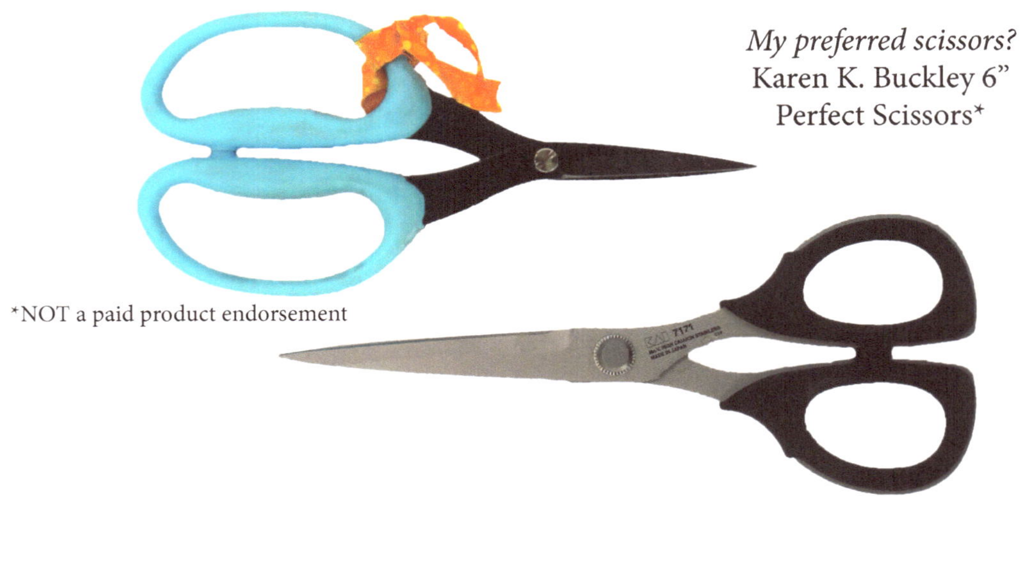

*NOT a paid product endorsement

DESIGN TEMPLATE

The templates in this book are designed to help you to easily identify changes in value. You will see that the simpler designs use fewer values than the more complex designs. As a design becomes more complex with a greater spectrum of values, it becomes more challenging to select fabric for those projects.

Keep this in mind if you want to create your own templates! The challenge with creating your own templates is to have enough value changes that you don't lose the defining characteristics of the subject, while simultaneously not having superfluous values. Generally, I find that 4-5 values in an image is about all I want to deal with. A design that has 6 or more value changes becomes a very difficult project.

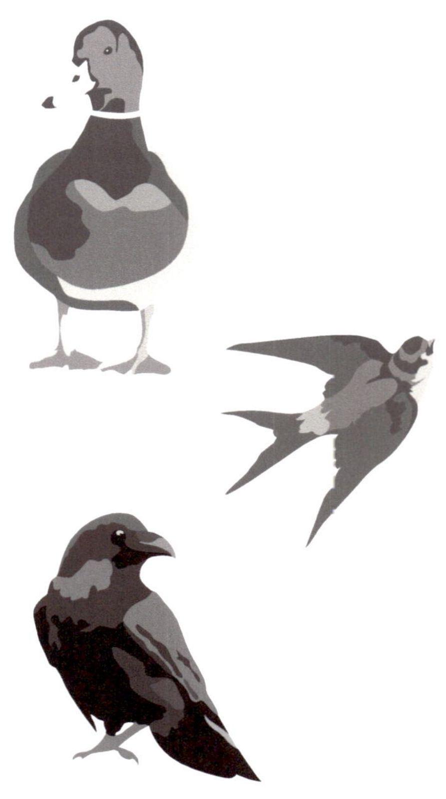

IRON & WOOL MAT

It is extremely helpful to use a mini iron, of the sort pictured here. The small size of the iron is helpful in pressing the first few pieces of fabric to the parchment paper. Additionally, if the SAS is not securely adhered to the back side of my fabric, having a small iron and wool pressing mat near my work station is useful for quickly pressing the SAS to my fabric again.

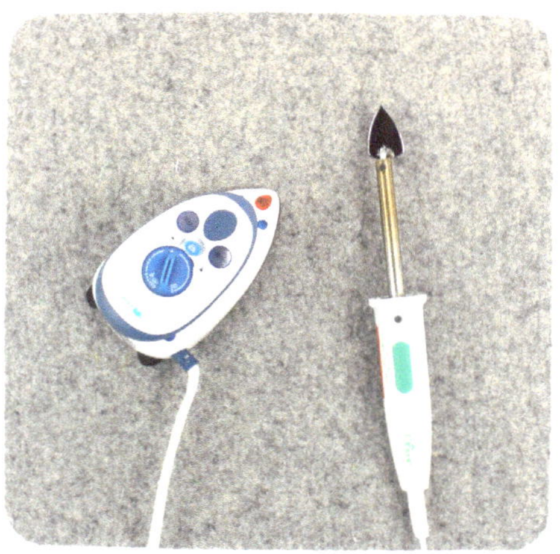

WORK SURFACE

A piece of 1/4" thick foam core covered in felt is the ideal surface for the projects in this book. Foam core can be purchased at a craft store in the framing department and can be cut to any size, although I recommend having a piece of foam core that's a minimum of about 20" x 20". Simply tape a piece of felt to the foam to protect it from the heat of an iron. The foam makes a sturdy but lightweight surface and allows me to use pins to hold the template and parchment paper in place.

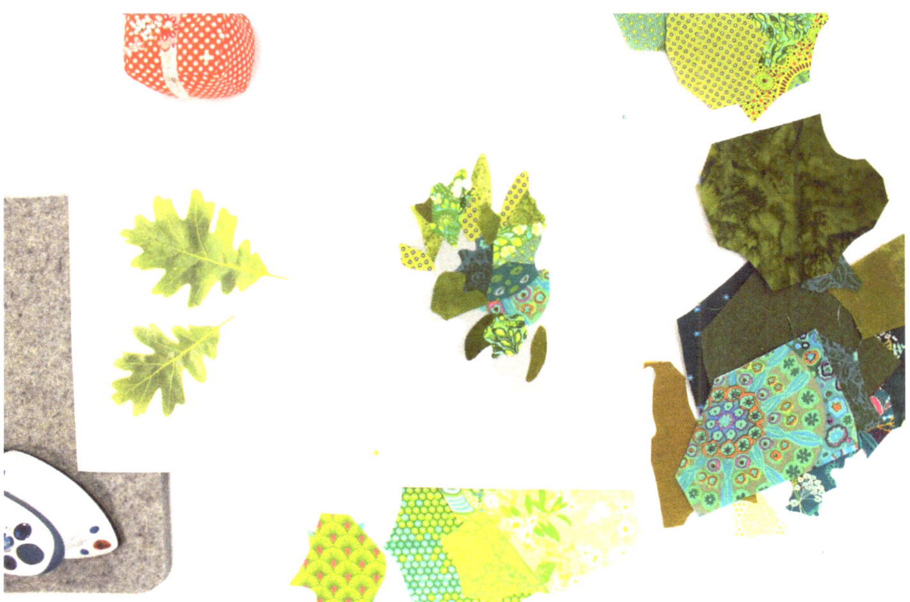

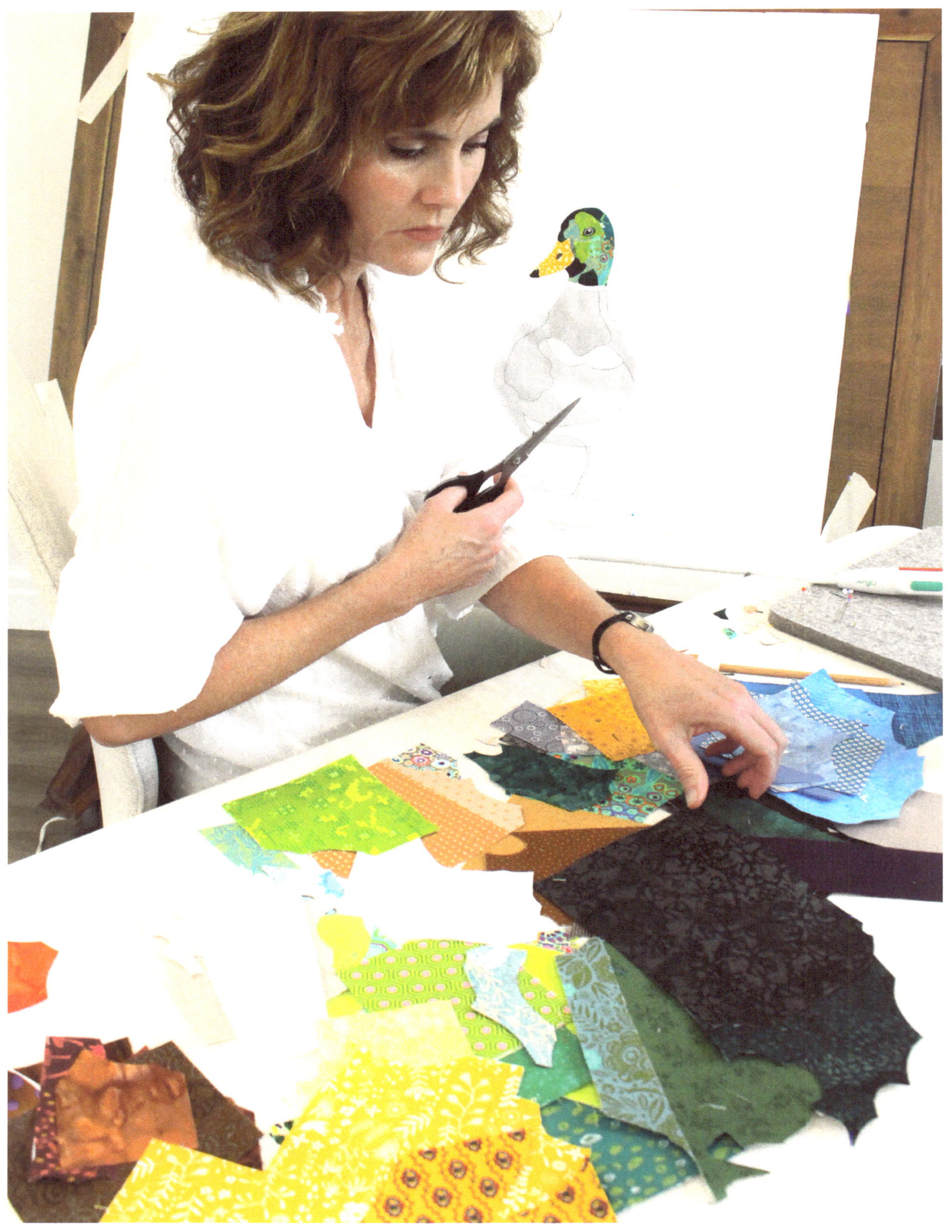

SELECT FABRIC

Sort According to Value

Select fabric for the design based on the number of values in the template.   For example, the Raven is a black bird, but the template has 4 values that I need to pay attention to. The changes in value are what give the bird depth and dimension, rather than looking flat. I begin by pulling a spectrum of fabric that ranges from very dark to light. I then sort the selected fabric into "value sets". A value set is a group of several fabrics that are very similar in value that I assign to a section of gray in the design.
The dark set includes very dark green, purple and blue fabrics. In fact, not one of my selected fabrics is solid black! For the lightest value set, rather than use exclusively light gray fabric choices, I incorporate light blue fabrics as well.

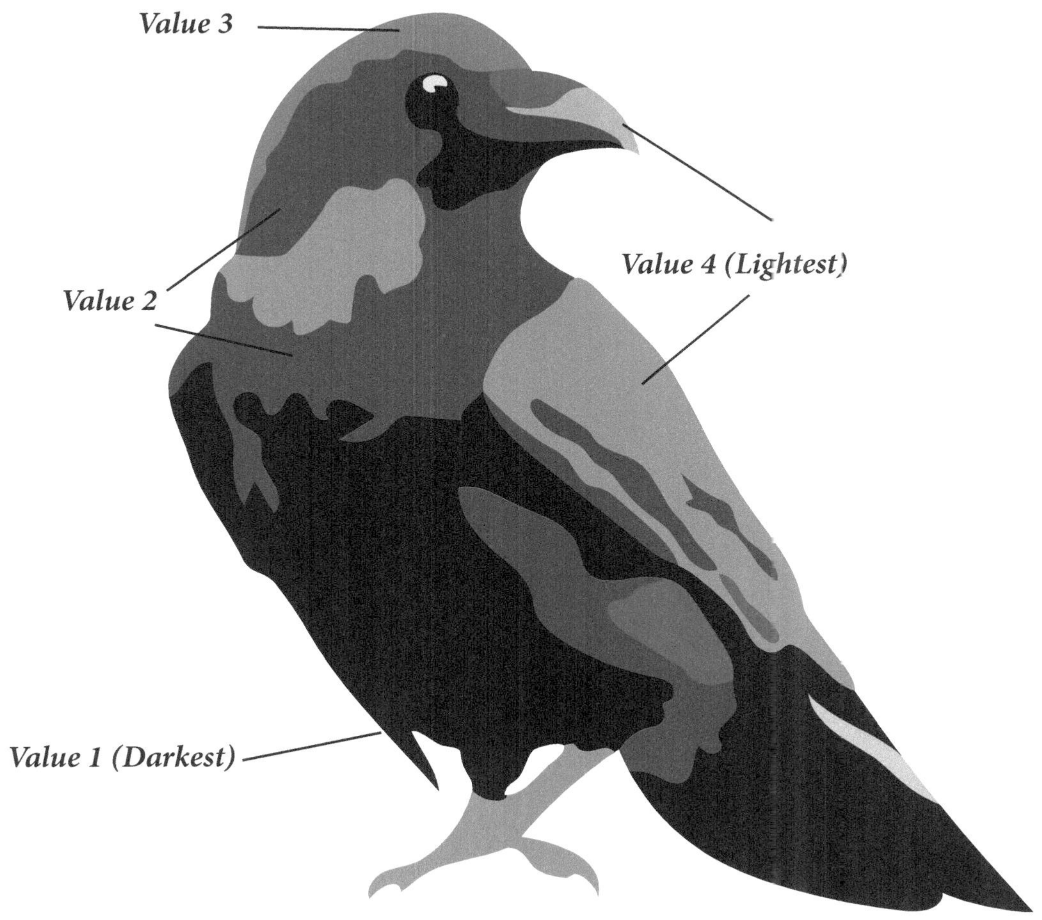

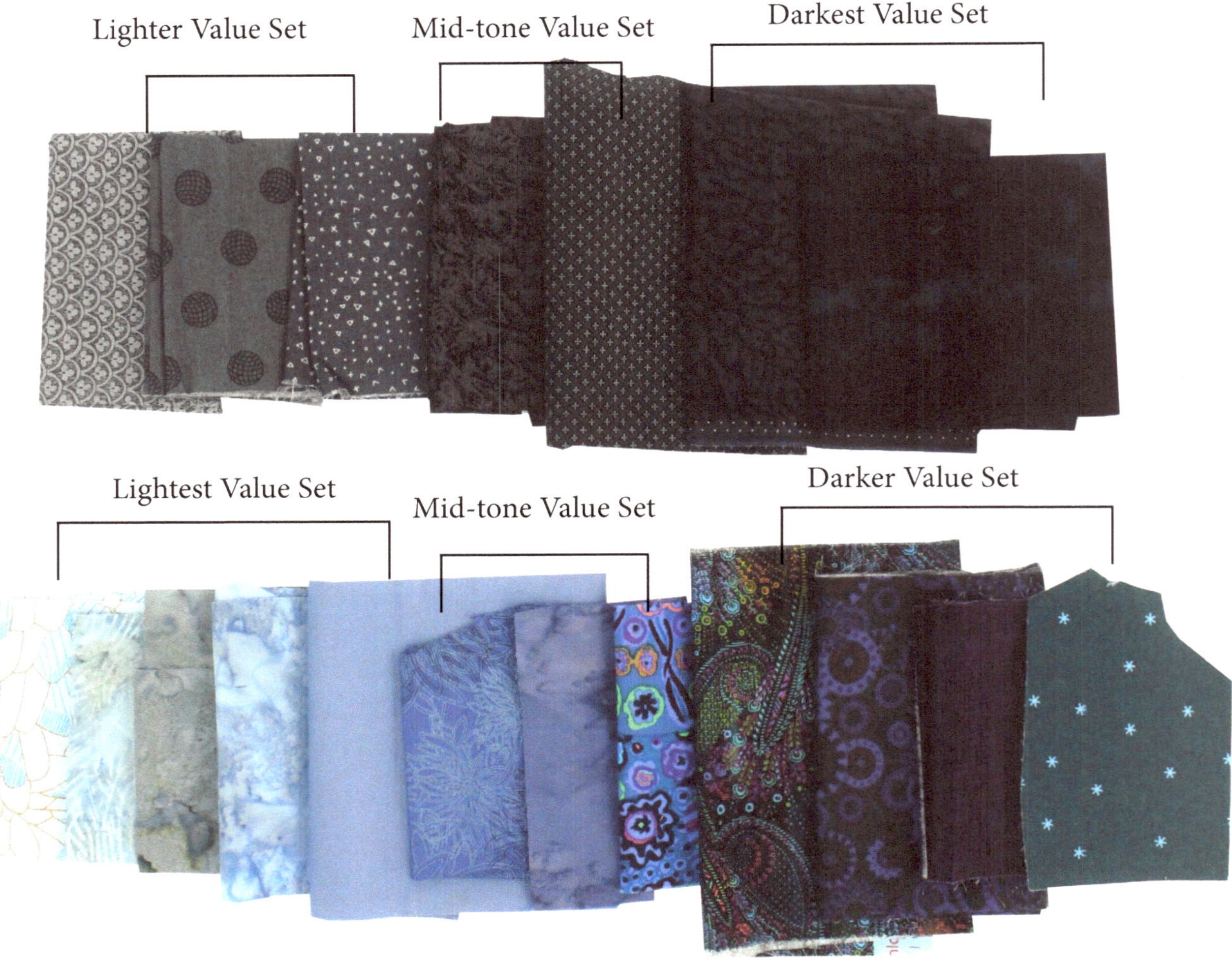

The gray guide is exactly that: a guide. The placement of fabric does not follow the shape of each value set precisely, and there are some fabrics in the mid-tones (the lighter and darker value sets) that cross over to the adjacent value.

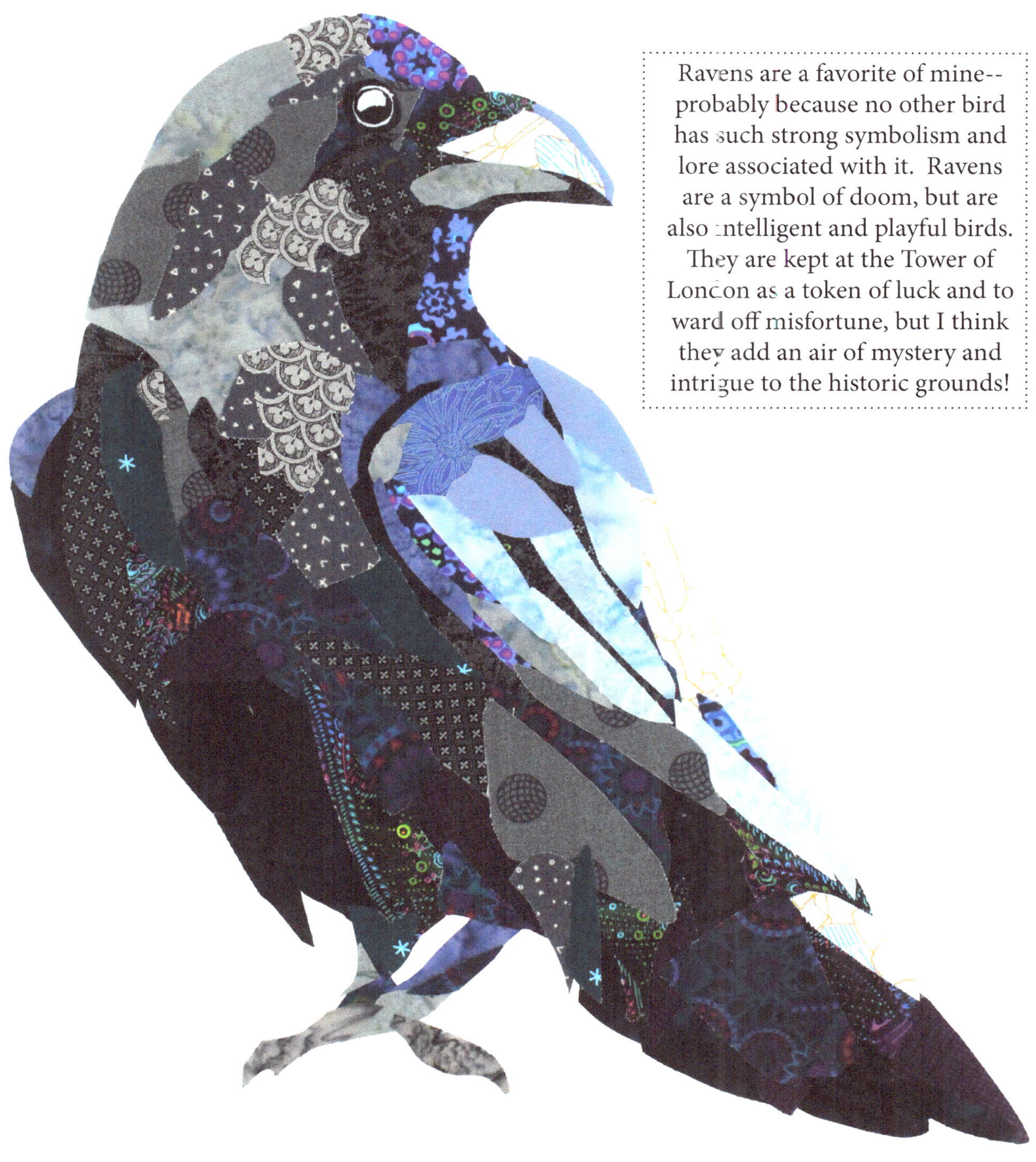

Ravens are a favorite of mine--
probably because no other bird
has such strong symbolism and
lore associated with it. Ravens
are a symbol of doom, but are
also intelligent and playful birds.
They are kept at the Tower of
London as a token of luck and to
ward off misfortune, but I think
they add an air of mystery and
intrigue to the historic grounds!

Why use so many different fabrics?

I prefer the look of multiple fabrics over the use of just a few. Multiple fabrics make each bird look more "painterly", as demonstrated in these two versions of the Swallow.

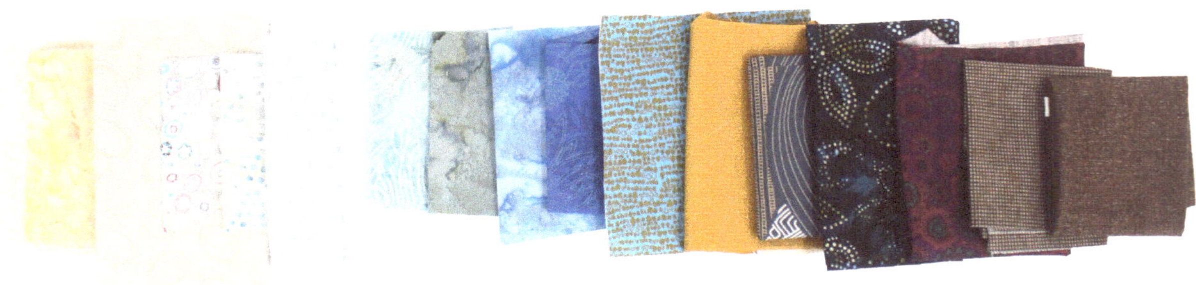

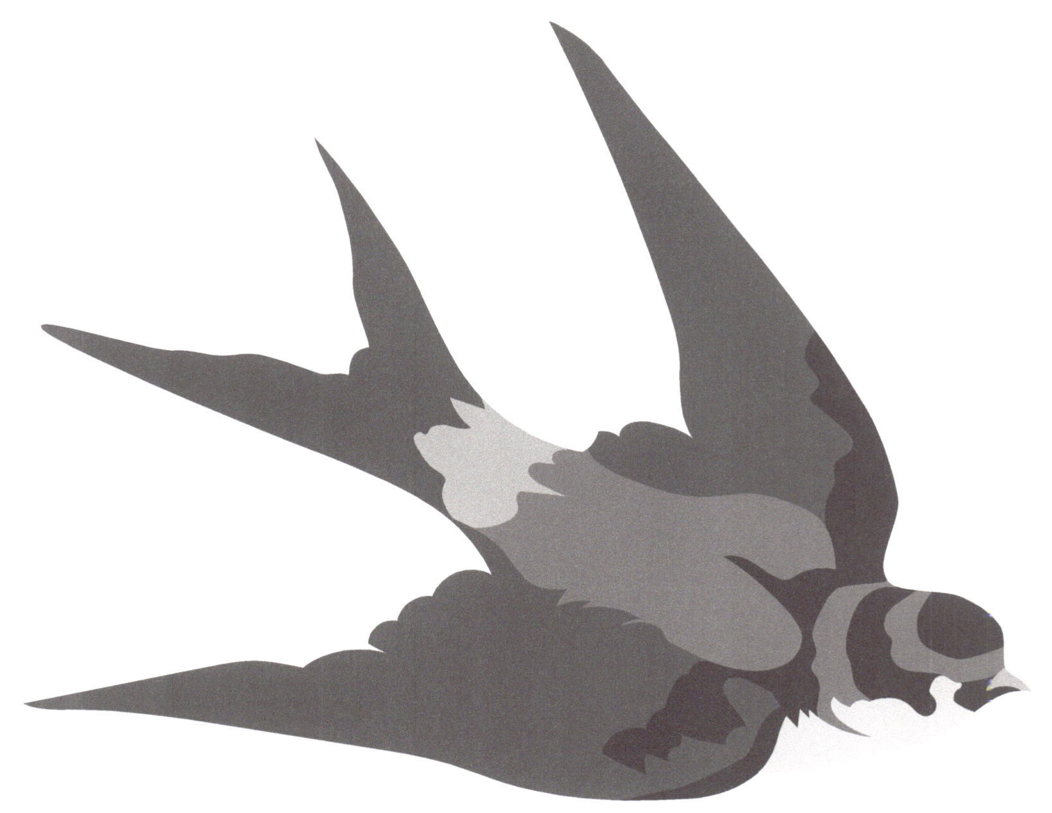

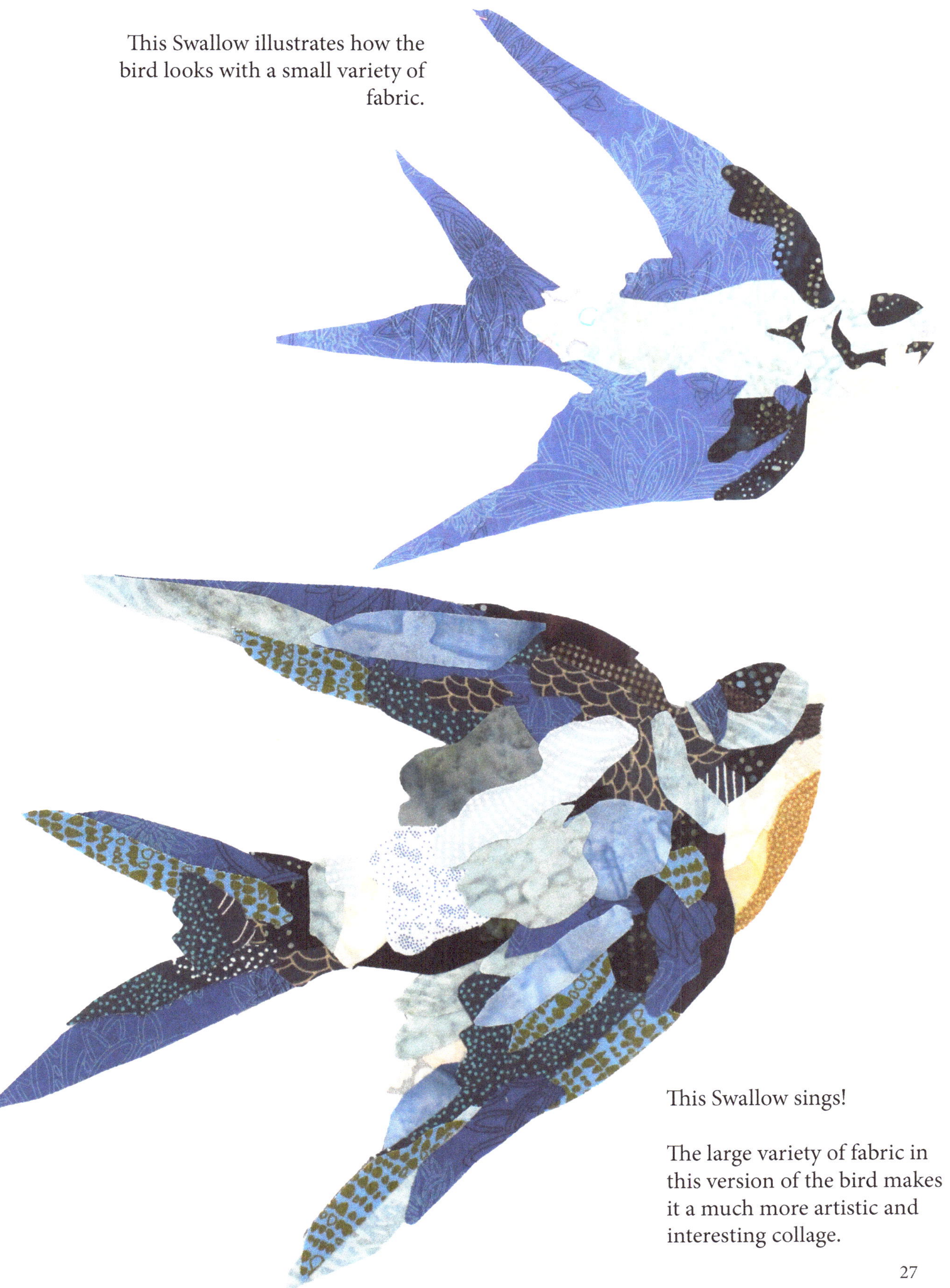

This Swallow illustrates how the bird looks with a small variety of fabric.

This Swallow sings!

The large variety of fabric in this version of the bird makes it a much more artistic and interesting collage.

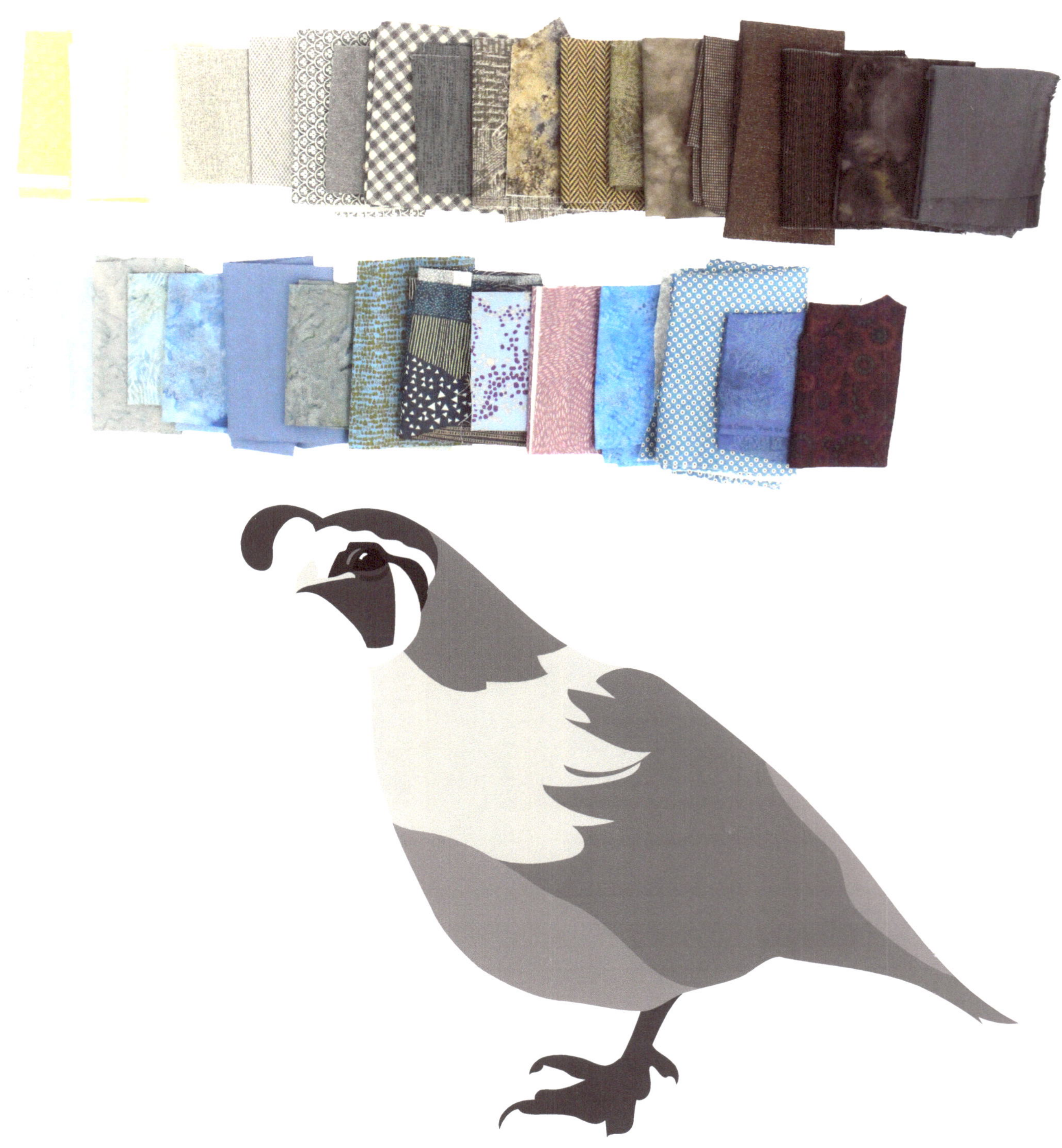

More Fabric = More Fun
Some of the fabric I select is only used in very small amounts, but I prefer to have an abundance of choices when I'm creating each collage.

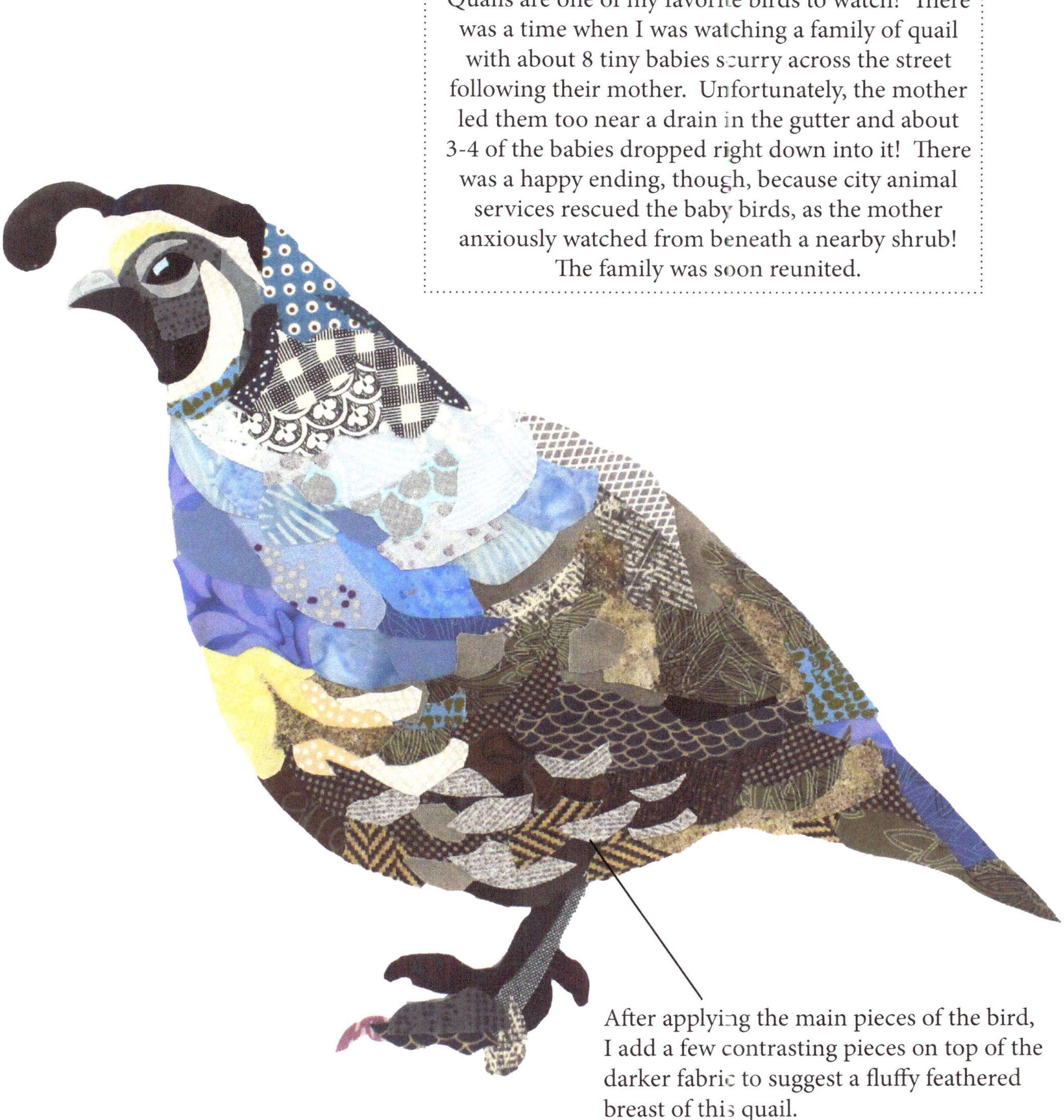

Quails are one of my favorite birds to watch! There was a time when I was watching a family of quail with about 8 tiny babies scurry across the street following their mother. Unfortunately, the mother led them too near a drain in the gutter and about 3-4 of the babies dropped right down into it! There was a happy ending, though, because city animal services rescued the baby birds, as the mother anxiously watched from beneath a nearby shrub! The family was soon reunited.

After applying the main pieces of the bird, I add a few contrasting pieces on top of the darker fabric to suggest a fluffy feathered breast of this quail.

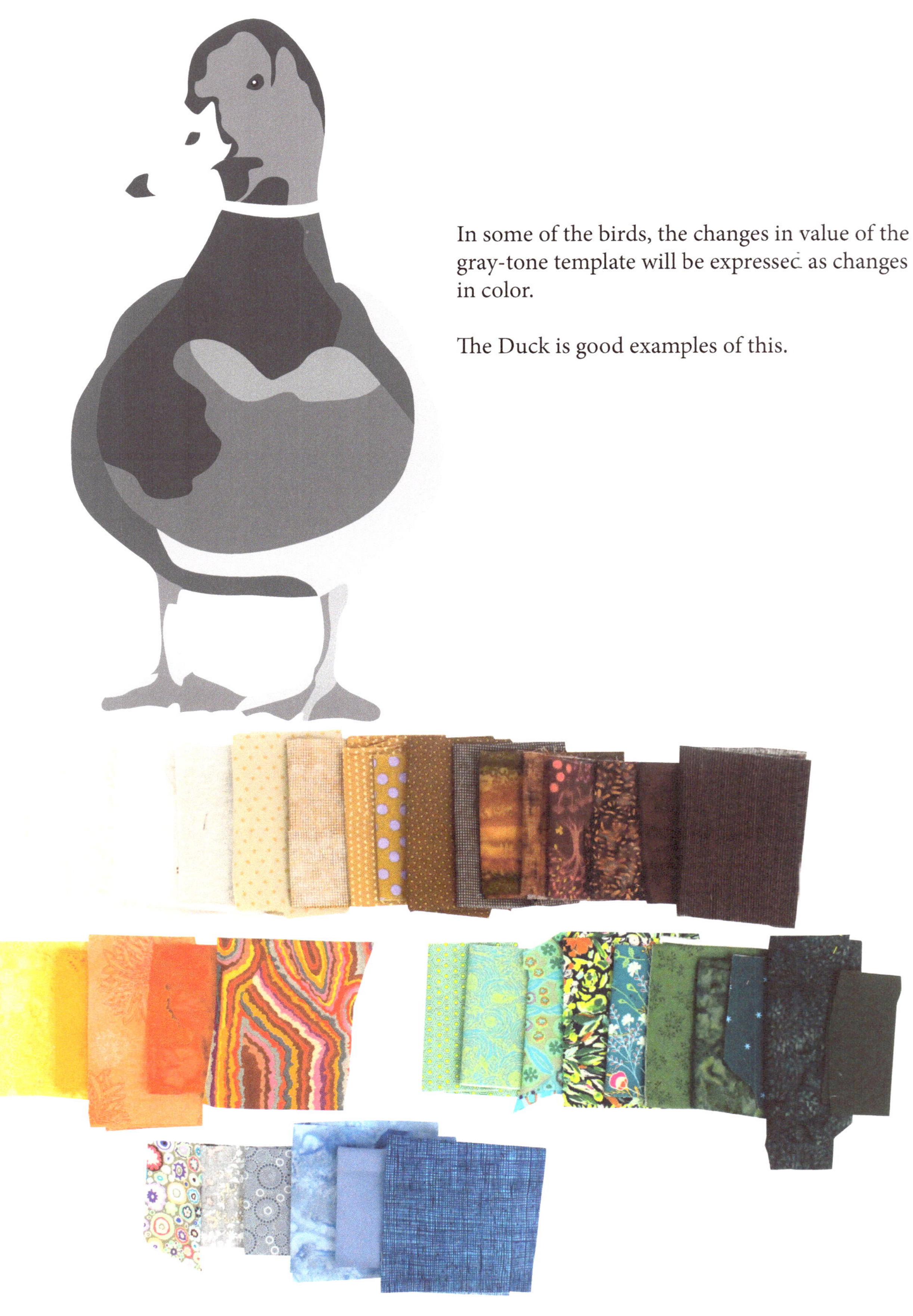

In some of the birds, the changes in value of the gray-tone template will be expressed as changes in color.

The Duck is good examples of this.

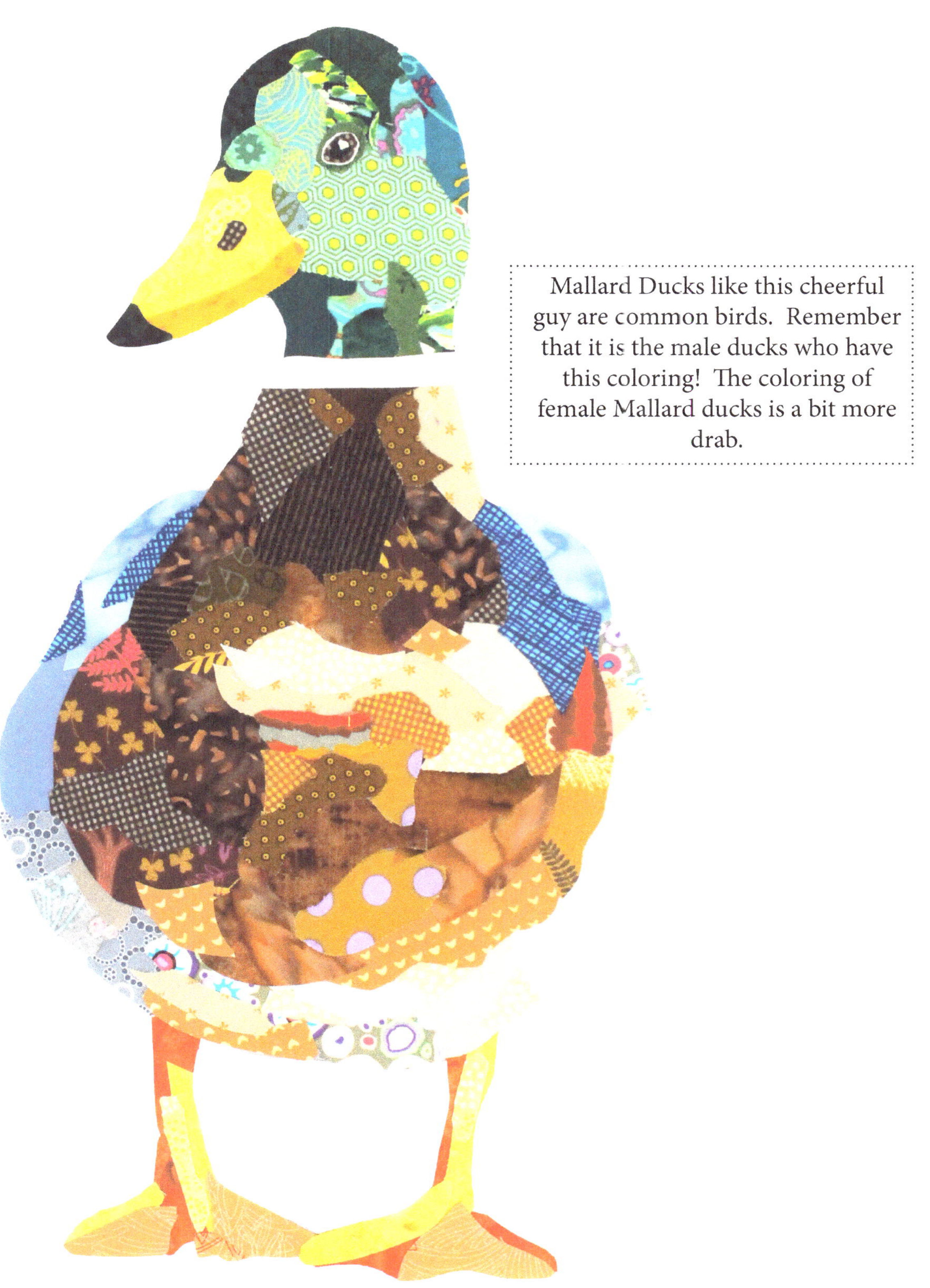

Mallard Ducks like this cheerful guy are common birds. Remember that it is the male ducks who have this coloring! The coloring of female Mallard ducks is a bit more drab.

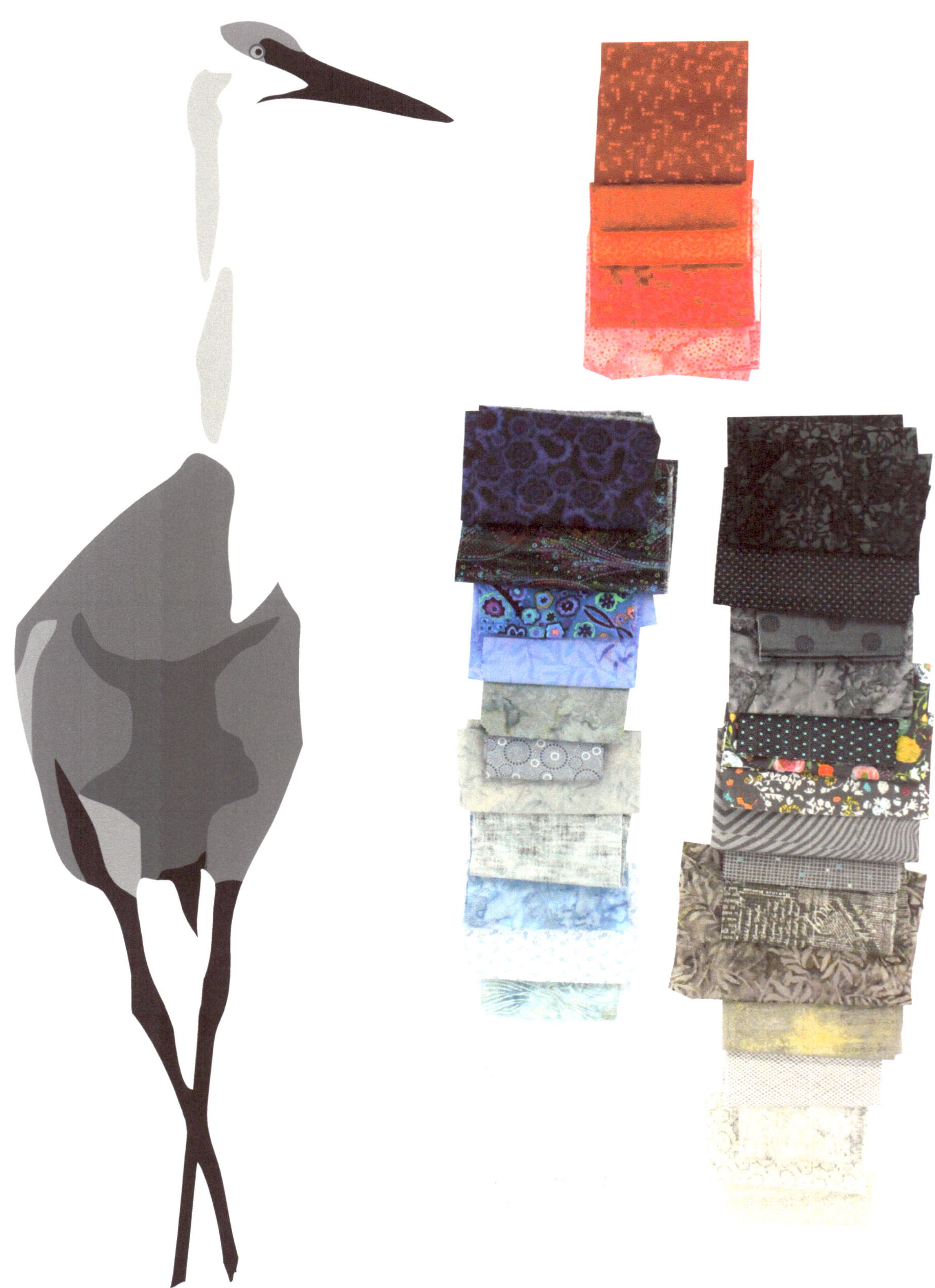

This selection of fabric is a good illustration of cool fabrics (left) and warmer fabrics (right).

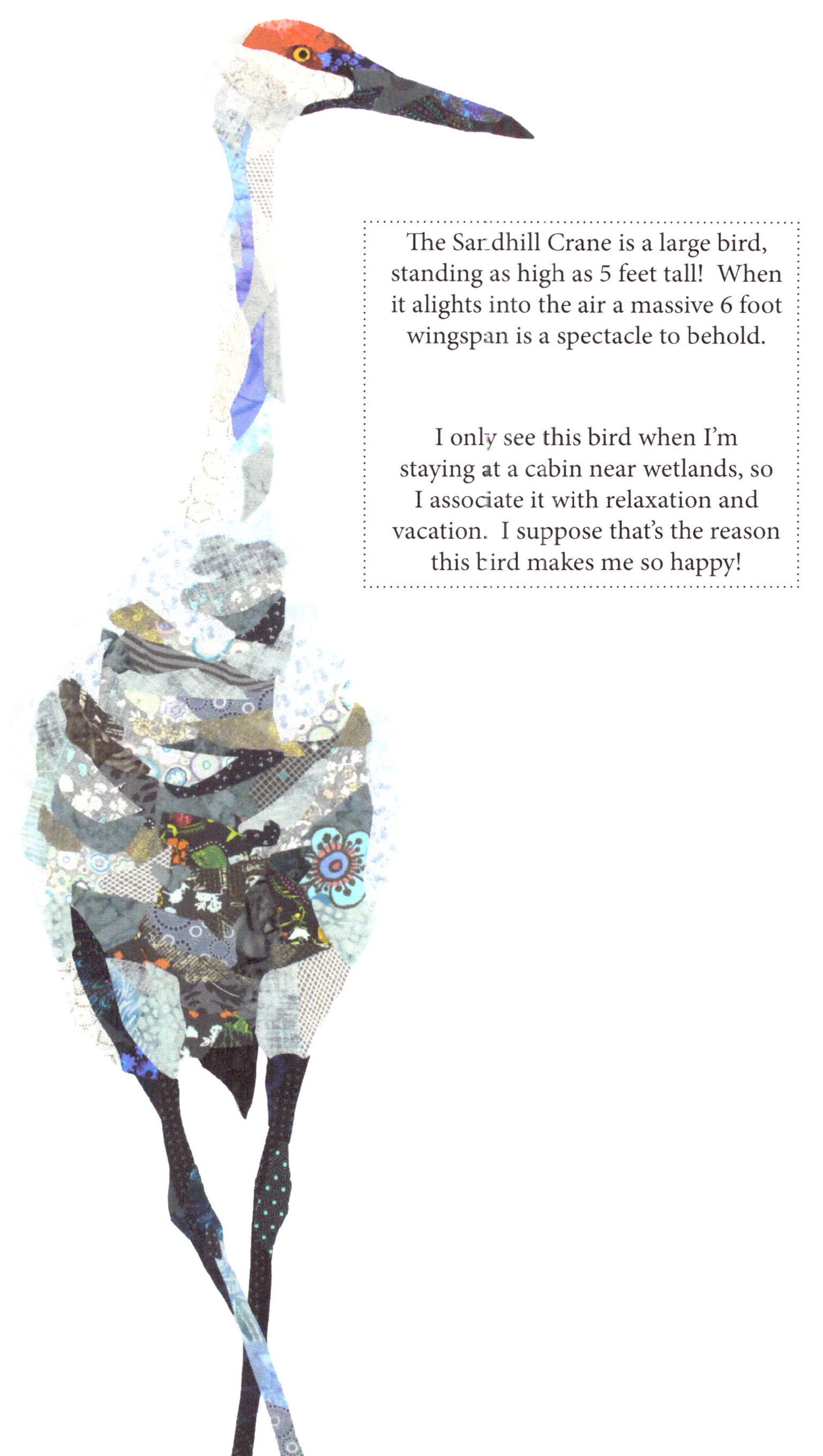

The Sandhill Crane is a large bird, standing as high as 5 feet tall! When it alights into the air a massive 6 foot wingspan is a spectacle to behold.

I only see this bird when I'm staying at a cabin near wetlands, so I associate it with relaxation and vacation. I suppose that's the reason this bird makes me so happy!

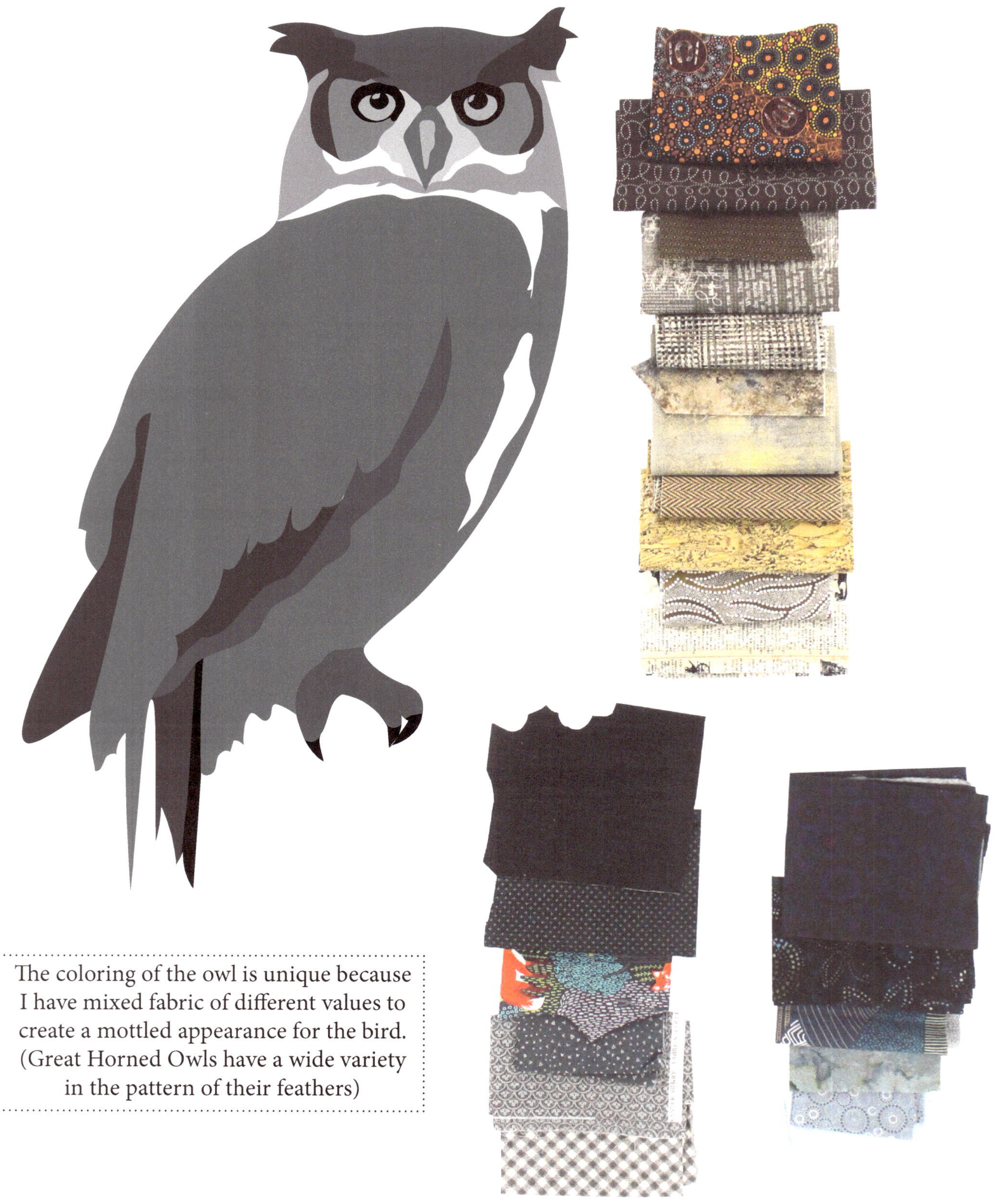

The coloring of the owl is unique because
I have mixed fabric of different values to
create a mottled appearance for the bird.
(Great Horned Owls have a wide variety
in the pattern of their feathers)

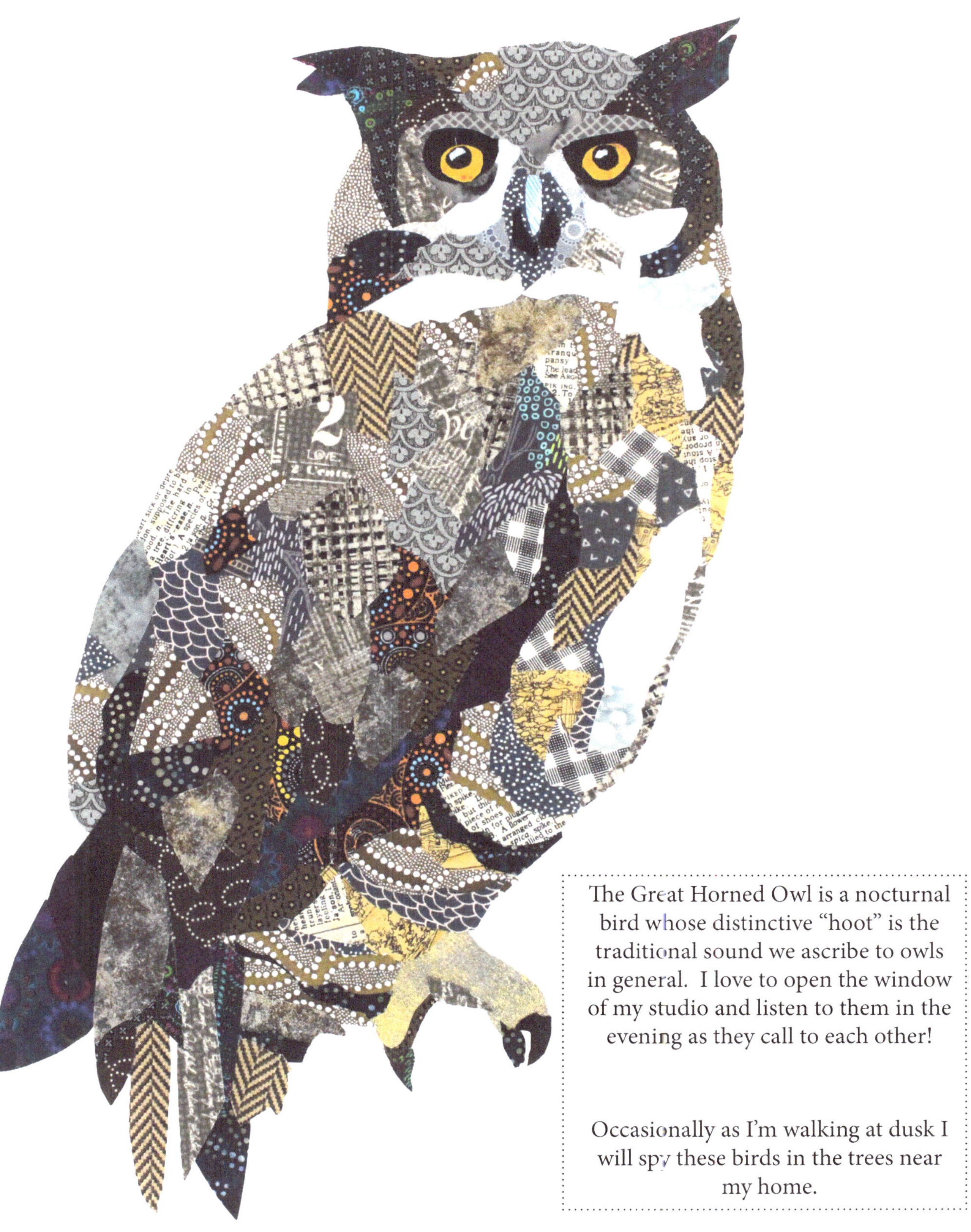

The Great Horned Owl is a nocturnal bird whose distinctive "hoot" is the traditional sound we ascribe to owls in general. I love to open the window of my studio and listen to them in the evening as they call to each other!

Occasionally as I'm walking at dusk I will spy these birds in the trees near my home.

PREPARE FABRIC

After I have selected the fabric that I want to use in my textile collage, I prepare my fabric with the SAS by cutting a rectangle of about 4.5" x 8" from an 1/8-yard strip. This is the advantage of cutting fabric in 1/8 yard increments! I like to be able to make a single cut from the strip and prepare it with the SAS. The remaining fabric is then easily folded up and stored in a shoe-box-size container.

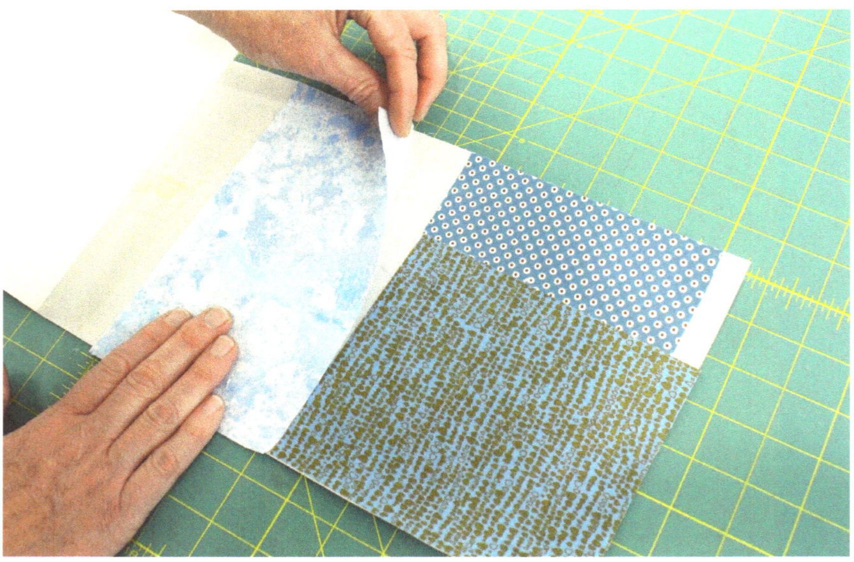

Here, I have peeled off the plain paper side of the SAS and I'm sticking my fabric pieces to the SAS. Once I've cut each piece of fabric, I'll lightly press the fabric (with a dry iron) to secure the fusible to the back. Now my fabric is ready to use!

PRINT THE TEMPLATE

I prepare the template of the bird by printing it at the size I choose at my local print and copy shop. Once I've had the template printed, I cut a piece of parchment paper to cover the entire template. I pin the template with the overlapping parchment paper to the work surface so that it is secure.

The images on pages 82-88 are to meant to be reproduced by a copy shop to the size that you want to create. However, if you prefer to download the full size images to send to your local shop, please scan this code for access to the original PDF files of each gray-tone template in this book.

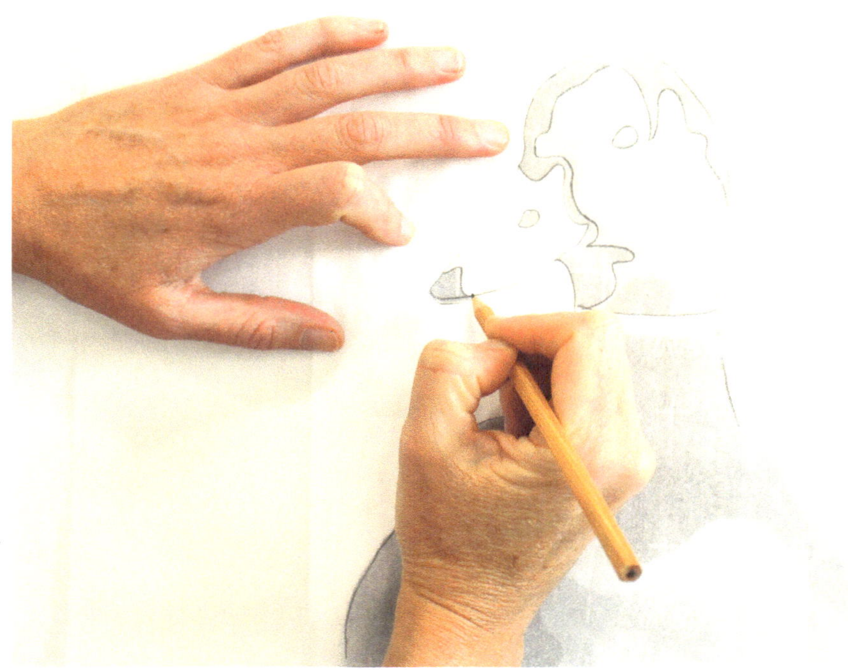

It's helpful to trace the template in pencil on the parchment paper, to better delineate where the values change in the design. The values of the template guide fabric selection and fabric placement, so it's important to understand where they change. Adding numbers to each section of the tracing makes it even easier-- now it's just like painting by number with fabric!

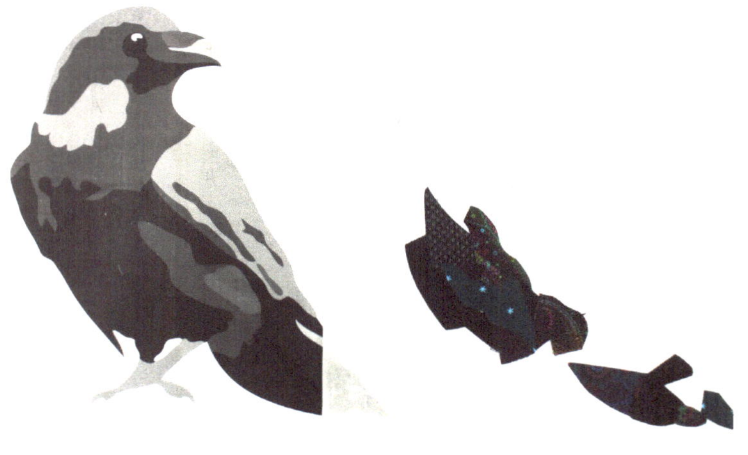

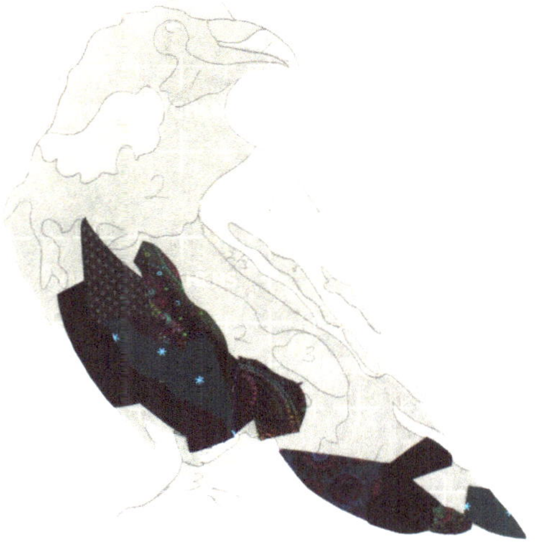

The reason that I use parchment paper, instead of simply applying fabric right to the template, is that I want to preserve the fusible so it's activated when I apply the finished bird to the background fabric of my project. Remember, that the fabric won't stick permanently to the parchment paper, like it would to the paper template!

APPLY FABRIC: PARCHMENT PRESSING

The "Parchment Pressing" method of fabric application enables me to create collaged elements of a larger piece independently from one another. This makes each design element less overwhelming than if I were to attempt the entire composition at the same time.

Additionally, making collage designs with the Parchment Pressing method gives me complete control over the size and composition of my project.

Now the fun begins! The most efficient shape is a triangle cut off the corner of a larger piece of fabric. I will generally round one or more of the edges of the triangle. (Rounded edges are easy to line up with the edges of most designs). The shape of the fabric pieces is not too critical~ my fabric pieces are quite random in shape.

A collage quilt can contain hundreds of individual pieces of fabric, so DO NOT obsess with the shape or placement of each piece fabric. Resist the urge to control the process of collage entirely, and allow the fabric to perform its magic. This will result in a more painterly and mature Impressionist look in your textile collage. Remember that we are striving for a good suggestion of our subject, not photo-realism.

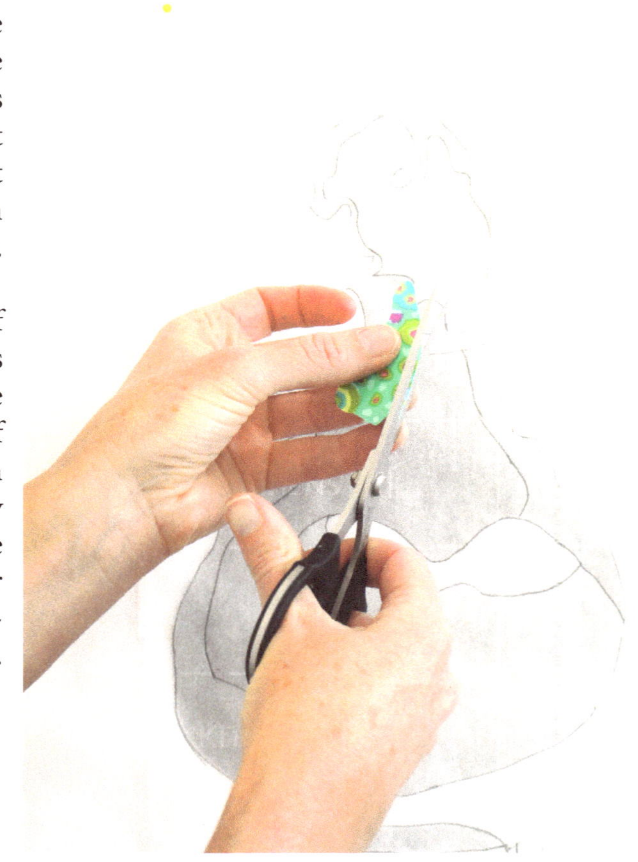

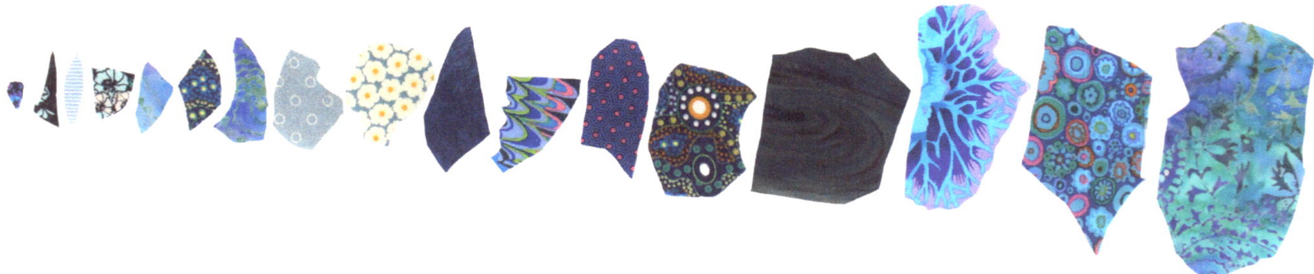

I try to keep the size of my fabric pieces no larger than the size of my palm and no smaller than my fingernail. When the section I'm working on is large, I increase the size of the pieces. When I'm working on a smaller section, or when I want to maintain detail, I will cut smaller pieces. I also only cut one or two pieces of fabric at a time.

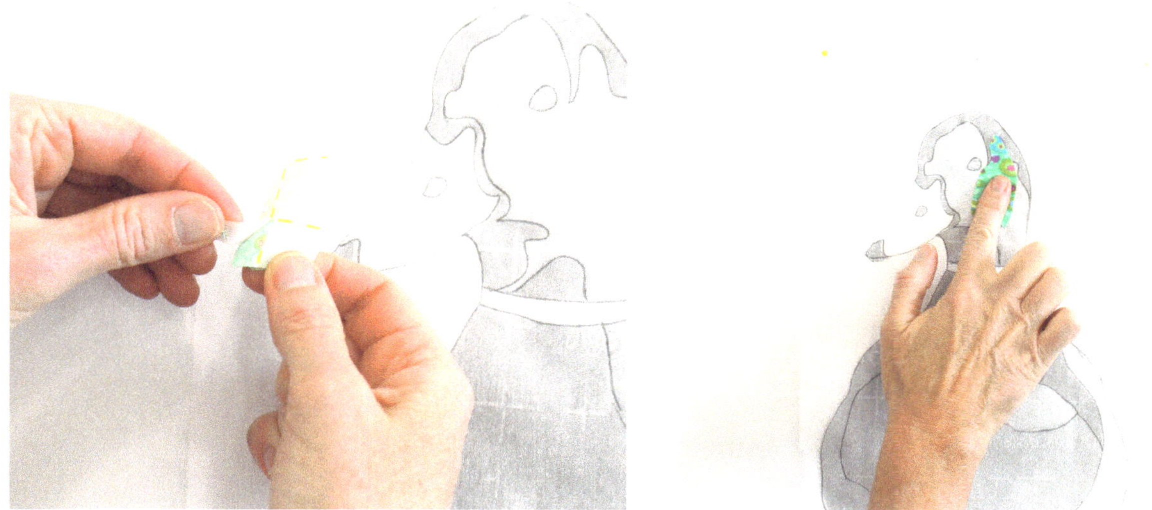

After cutting a piece of fabric, I score the paper on the back using a pin. This helps to peel away the paper easily and expose the sticky temporary adhesive on the back of the fabric. I place my fabric on the parchment paper, using the template and pencil-tracing as a guide.

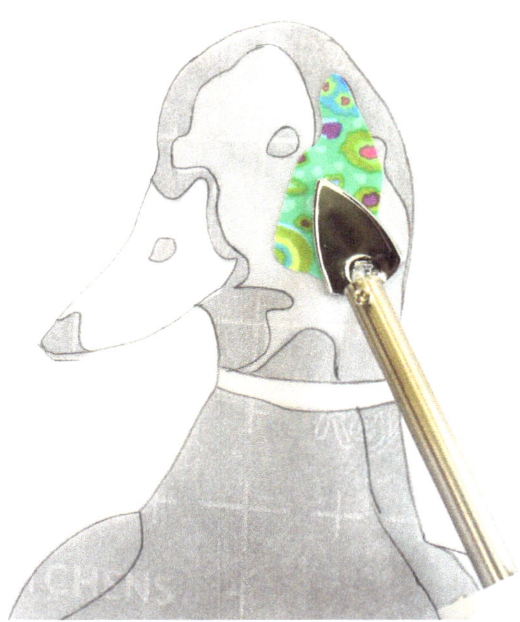

Because the parchment paper is designed to be a non-stick surface, it can be helpful to press the first few pieces of the collage with a hot iron to activate the adhesive. Just be careful not to use steam while the collage is still on the parchment paper!

I apply subsequent pieces so that they overlap each other by about 1/4". This overlap is important because the pieces will stick to each other and enable me to peel the entire finished piece off in one piece!

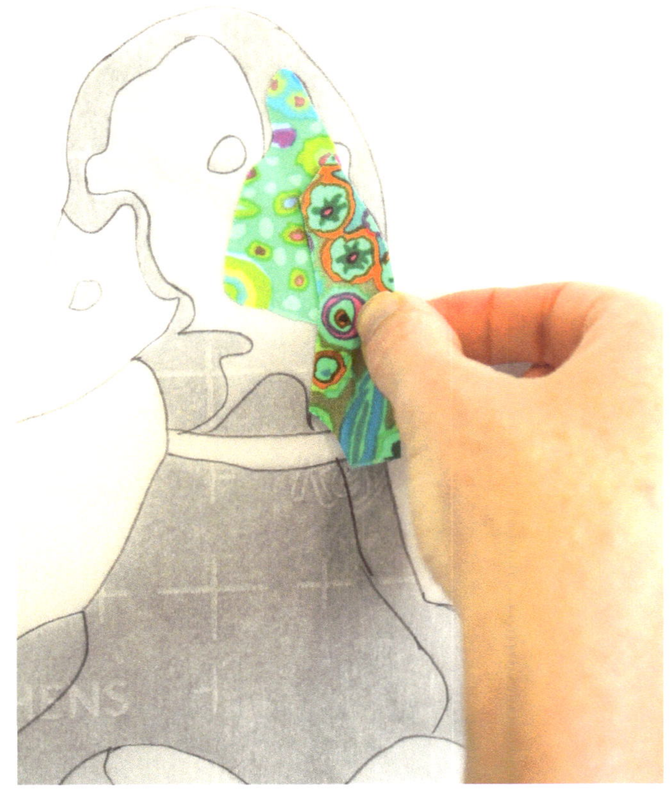

I make the fabric pieces fit in the area of the design I'm working on, but I don't worry too much about staying in the lines. It's a little bit like doing a puzzle (except I can cheat by cutting and overlapping the pieces)!

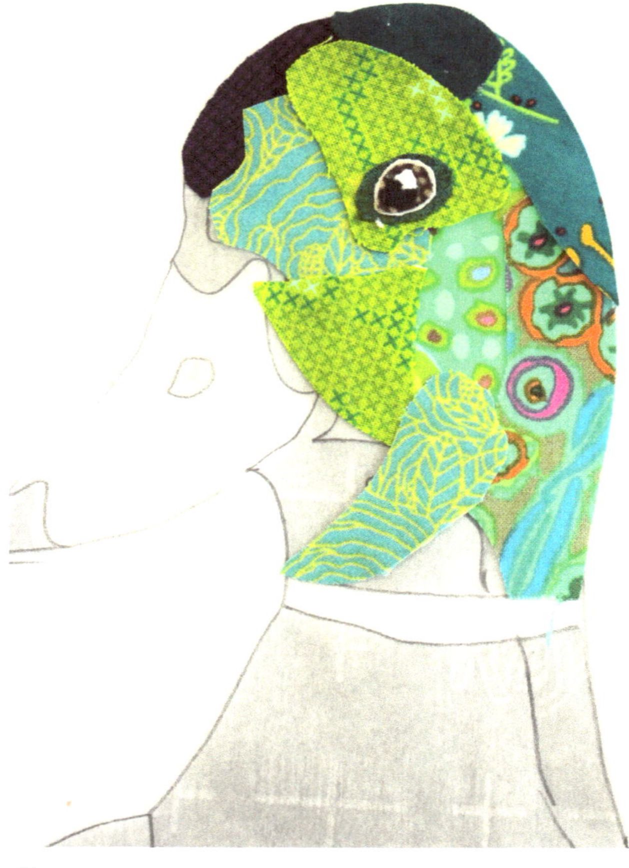

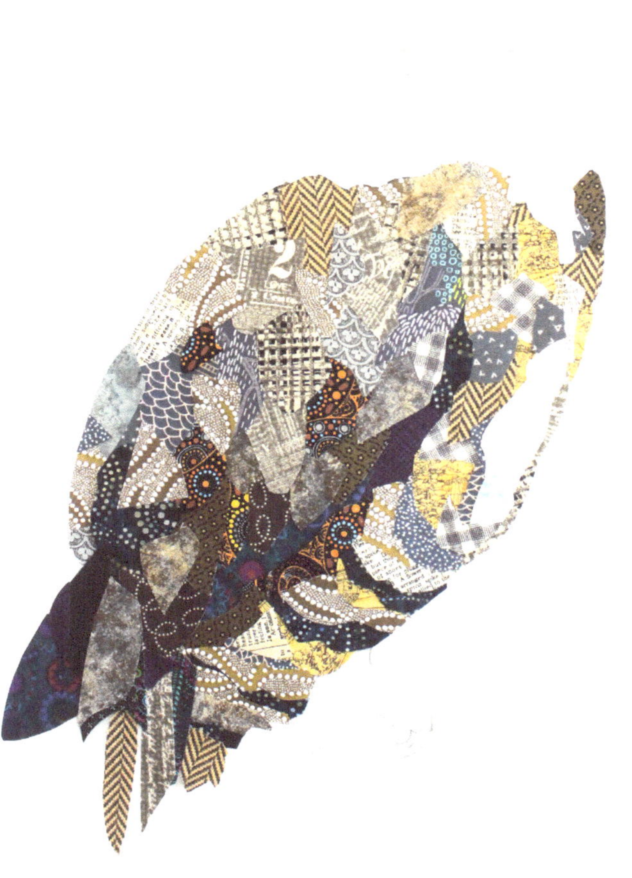

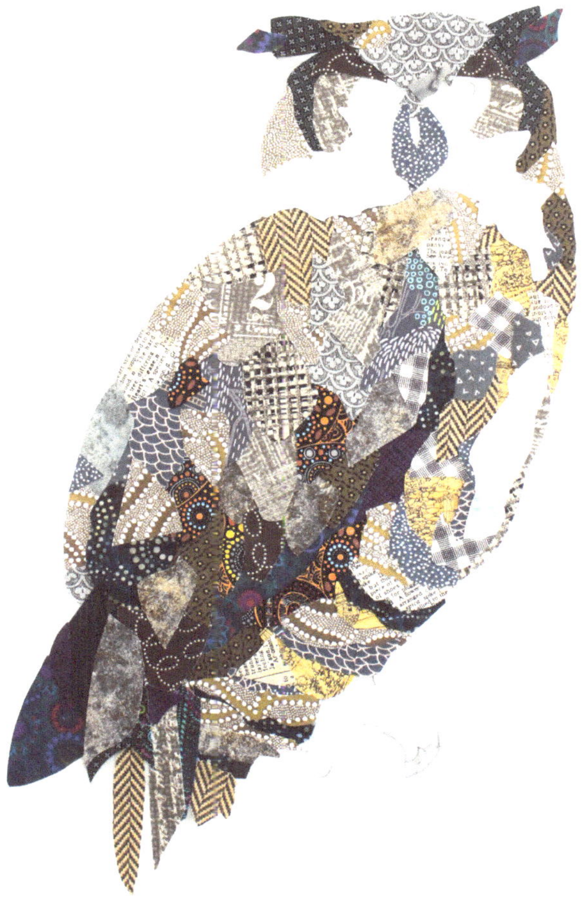

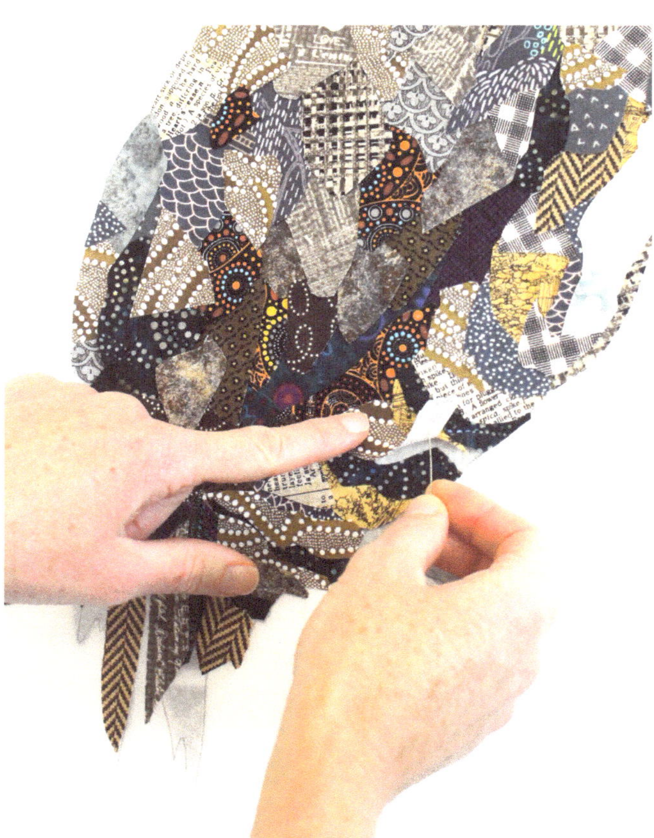

As I work, there will be occasional times when I want to replace a piece of fabric with something else. It's easy to do while the pieces are temporarily adhered to each other.   Simply use a pin to lift the fabric away from the parchment paper and replace the desired piece.

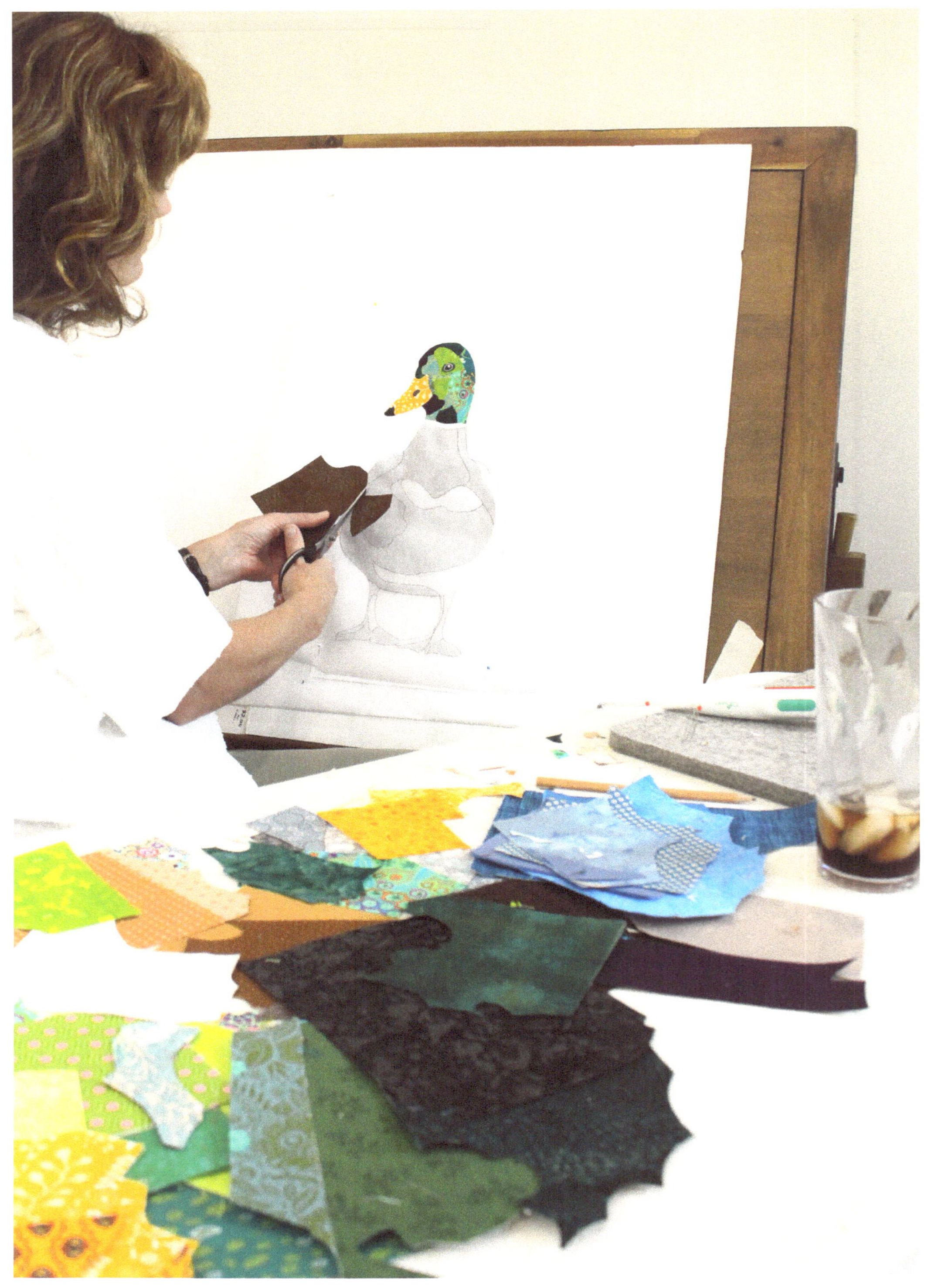

I continue to cut fabric pieces and apply them to the parchment paper until my collage is complete! When it's finished, I press the design with a hot, dry iron to fuse the pieces to each other. I leave the finished collaged element on the parchment paper until I'm ready to use it in a larger composition or project.

There are times when I want to be more precise in the placement of fabric pieces. To create eyes, for instance, I need to be able to define smaller and more intricate details. A tracing of the template onto the SAS paper provides gives me this ability.

The eyes of these birds are simple to make, but look complex and provide a sophisticated touch to our feathered friends. I'll demonstrate the process with both the duck and the owl.

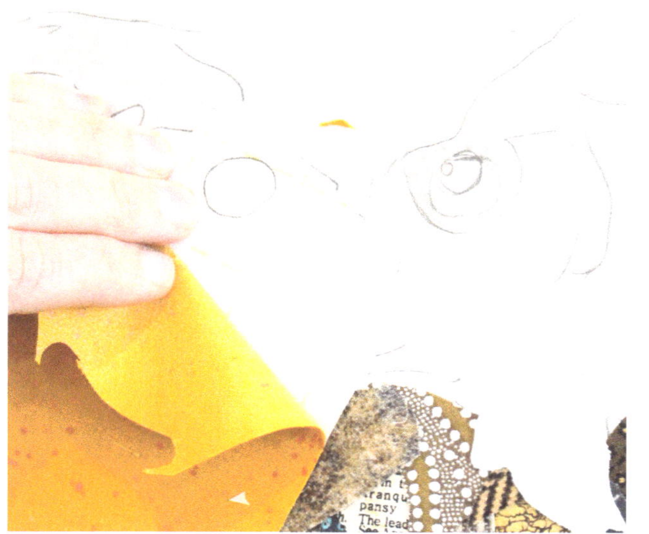

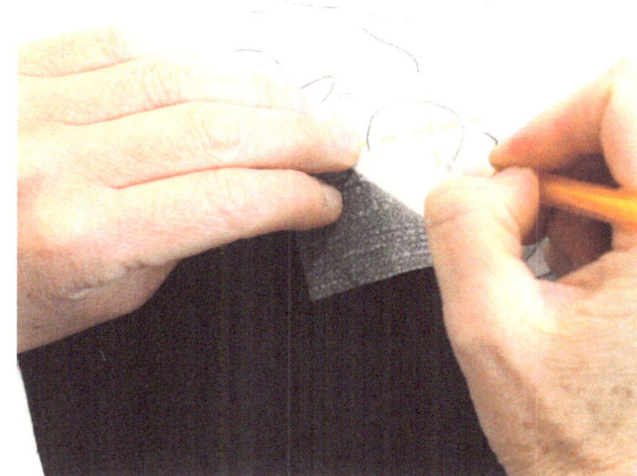

One Peel back the paper from the fusible on the back side of the selected fabric and trace the eye with a pencil.

The eyes of the owl have a dark outer section, a yellow iris, and a black pupil, so I trace each section.

The duck has a simple dark eye.

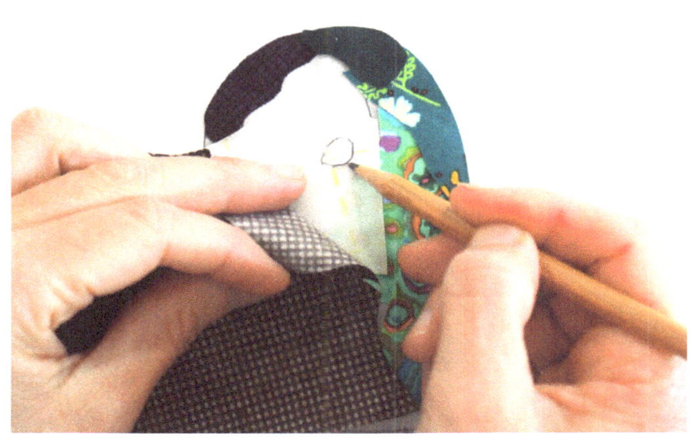

Use this "SAS Tracing" technique anywhere you want to be precise with the size and shape of your fabric pieces.

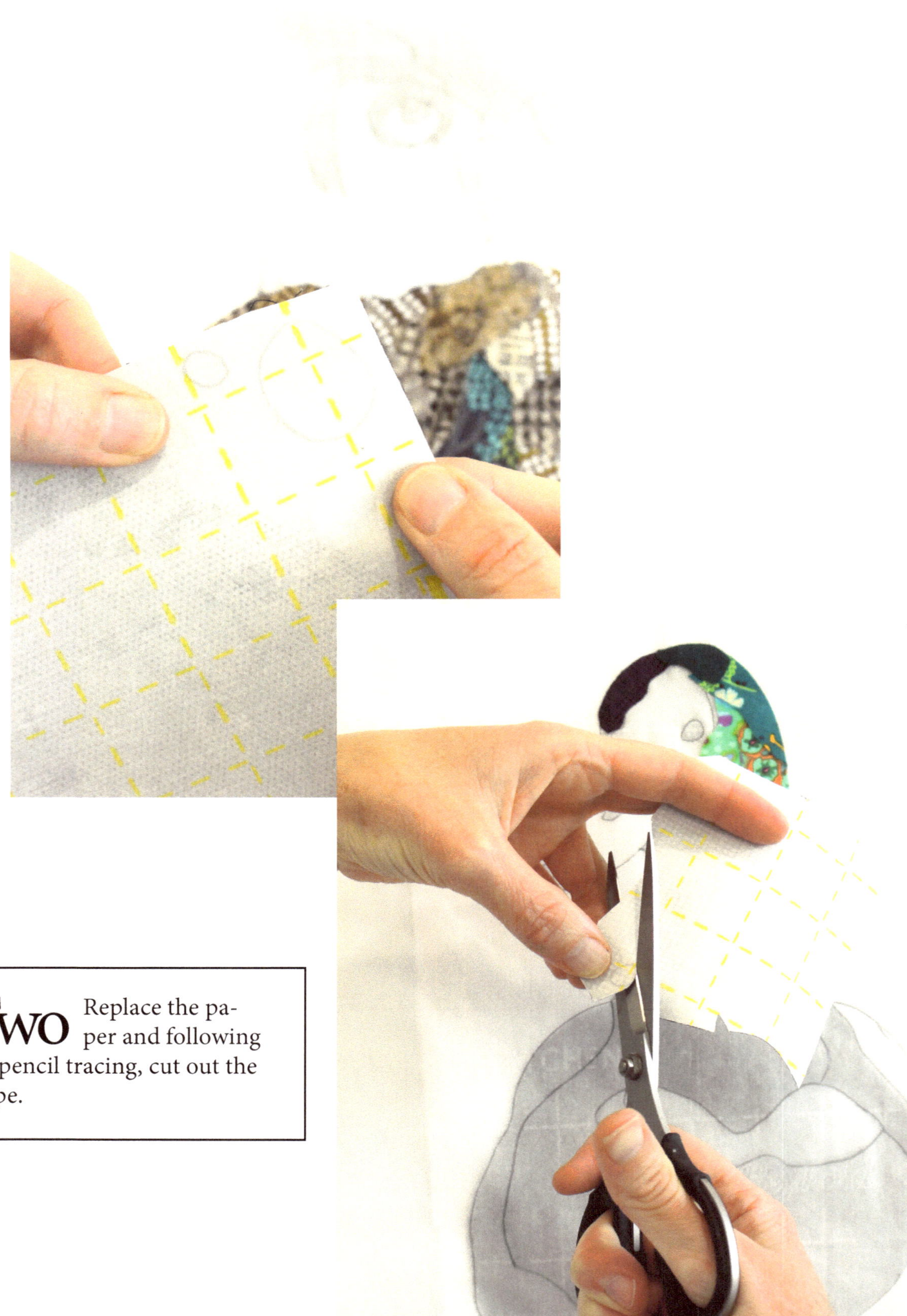

Two Replace the paper and following the pencil tracing, cut out the shape.

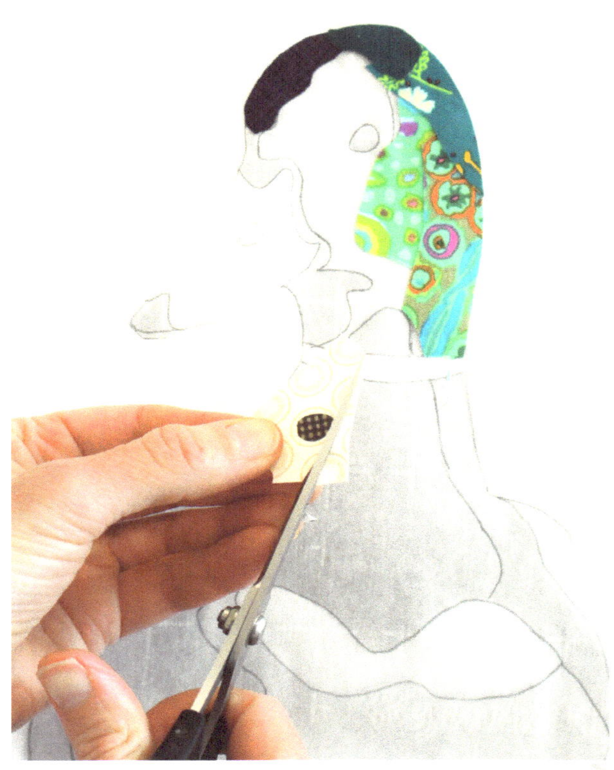

For the eye of the duck, lay the dark piece of fabric on top of a lighter piece and cut tightly around the shape. The lighter piece of fabric underneath the eye provides a scant highlight so that the eye stands out from the darker fabric beneath it.

Repeat this step for the eye of the duck. Place the layered eye onto a dark fabric and cut around it.

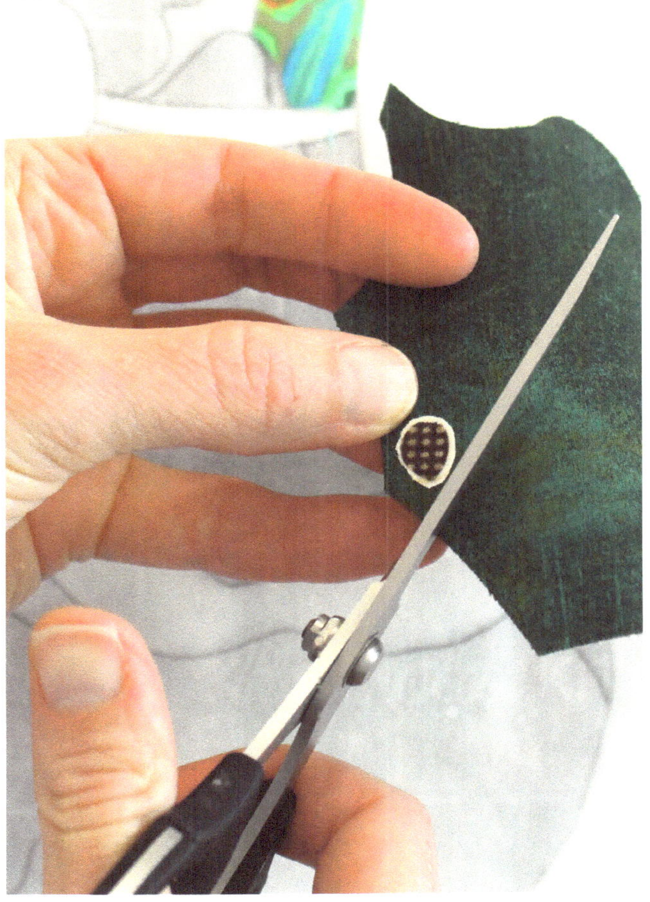

Three

Place the eye in position by following the template. Use a pin to lift fabric which may be covering the tracing.

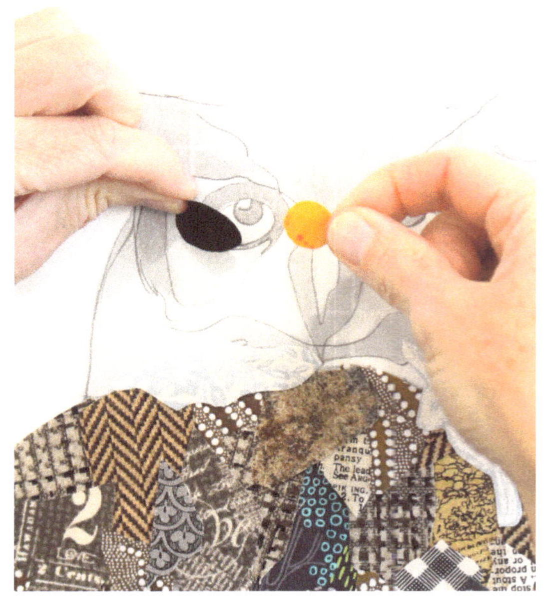

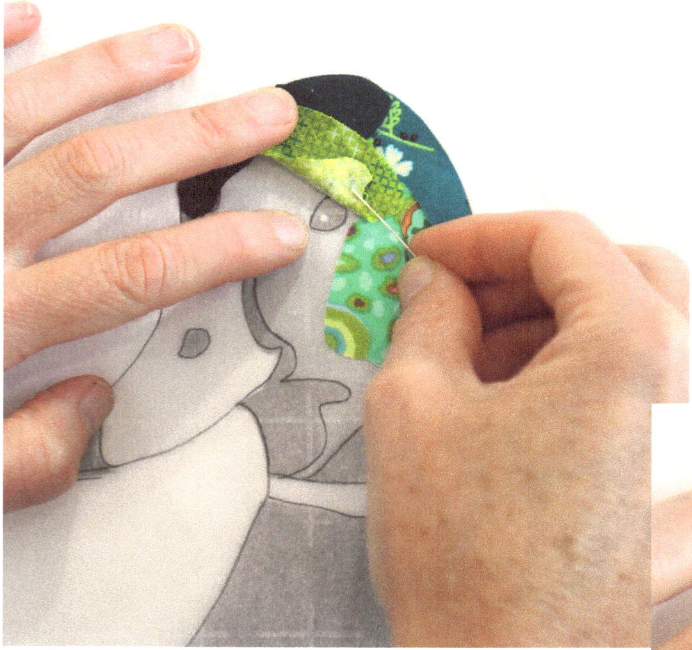

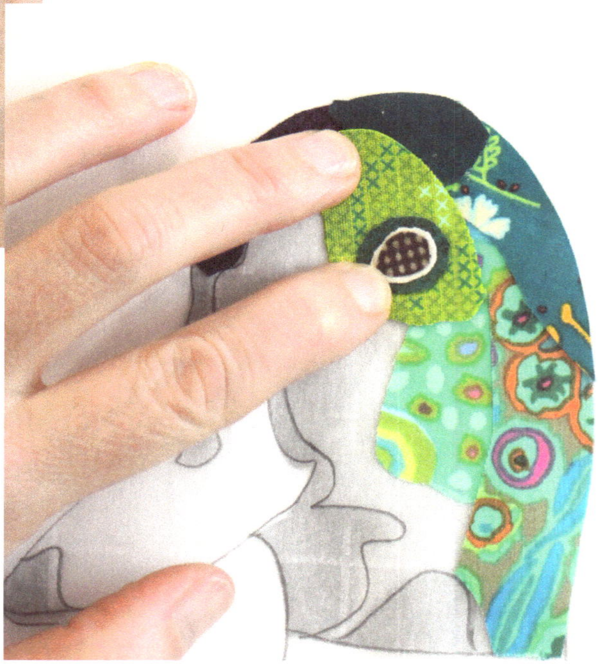

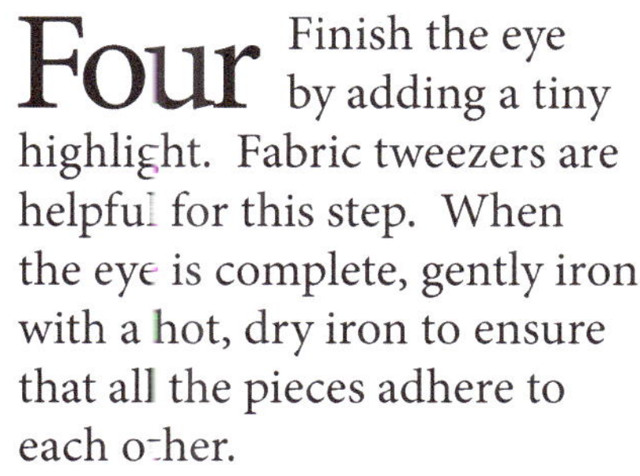

Four Finish the eye by adding a tiny highlight. Fabric tweezers are helpful for this step. When the eye is complete, gently iron with a hot, dry iron to ensure that all the pieces adhere to each other.

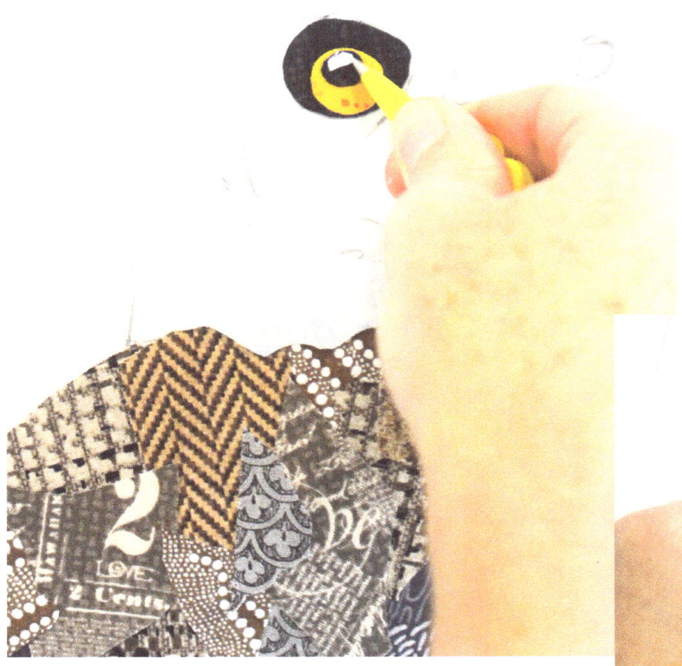

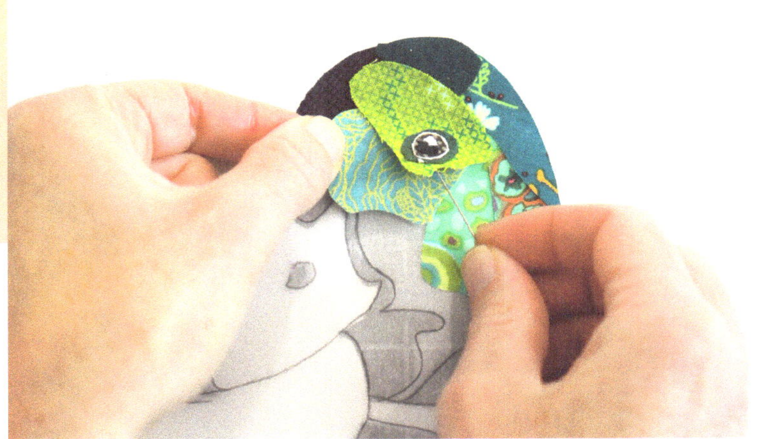

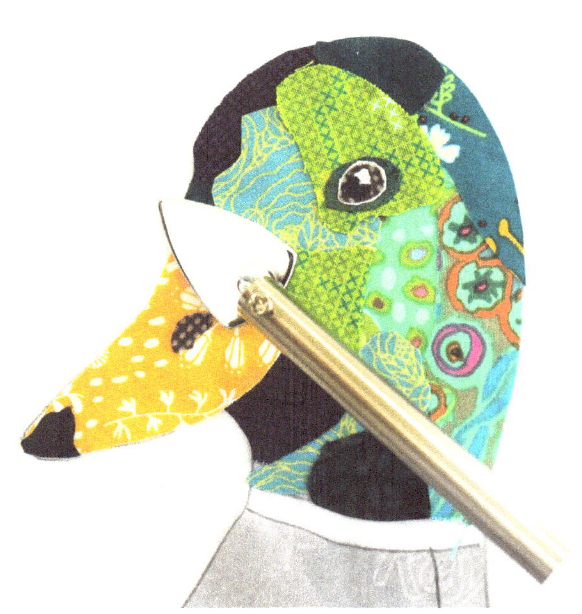

Complementary Design Elements

I have used a few additional "elements" or designs that complement the birds and help to provide some further context to the final composition. I've provided the gray-tone templates of some of them in the appendix.

I also created grasses and simple branch perches that are not in this book. To create additional ancillary design elements, simply draw a template of the desired element with pencil on parchment paper and collage the element. It helps to place the parchment paper over the bird for which you are creating the element. This way, the scale and placement of the element is accurate.

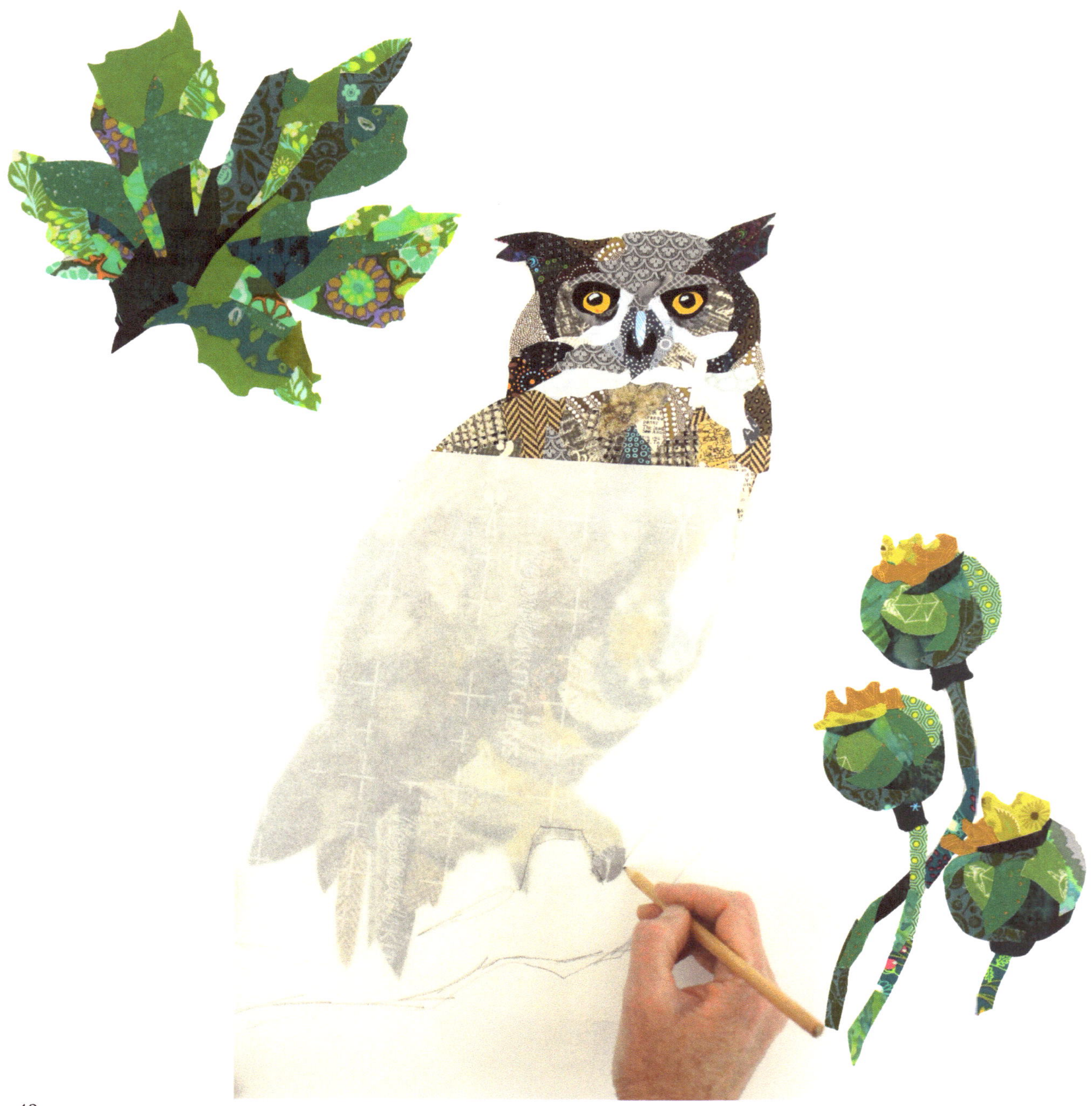

When I have completed each of the elements that I want to include in my project, it's time to pull things together! There are a few principles to consider when composing the final piece to ensure that it's pleasing to look at. I like to group the principles into three categories: harmony, balance and scale.

HARMONY

Harmony is achieved when the layout of the piece "feels just right", or when it "works". This concept can apply to the relationships between each element in the piece, as well as to color in a composition.

Remember the number *three* when creating harmony. Think in groupings of three and the Rule of Thirds. The Rule of Thirds states that an arrangement of three (or thirds) makes the most aesthetically pleasing formation.

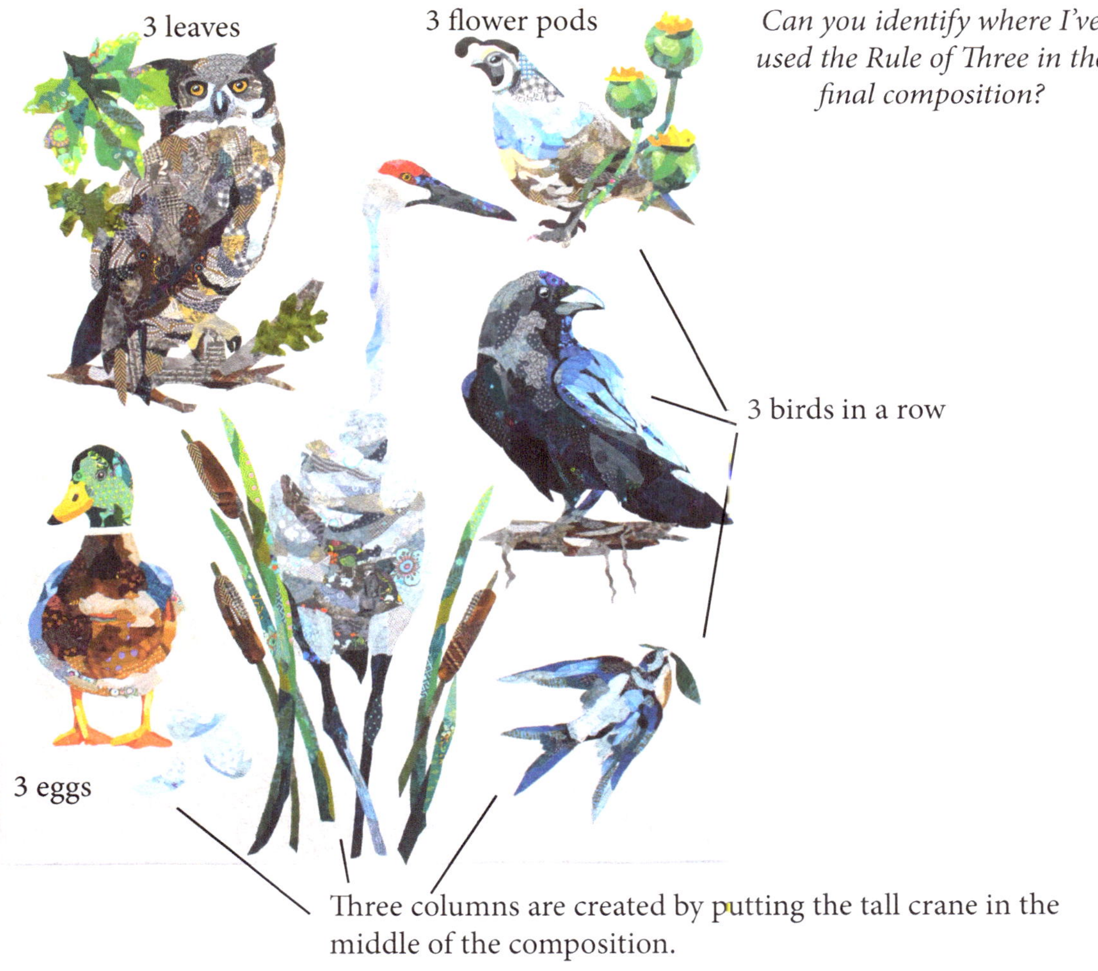

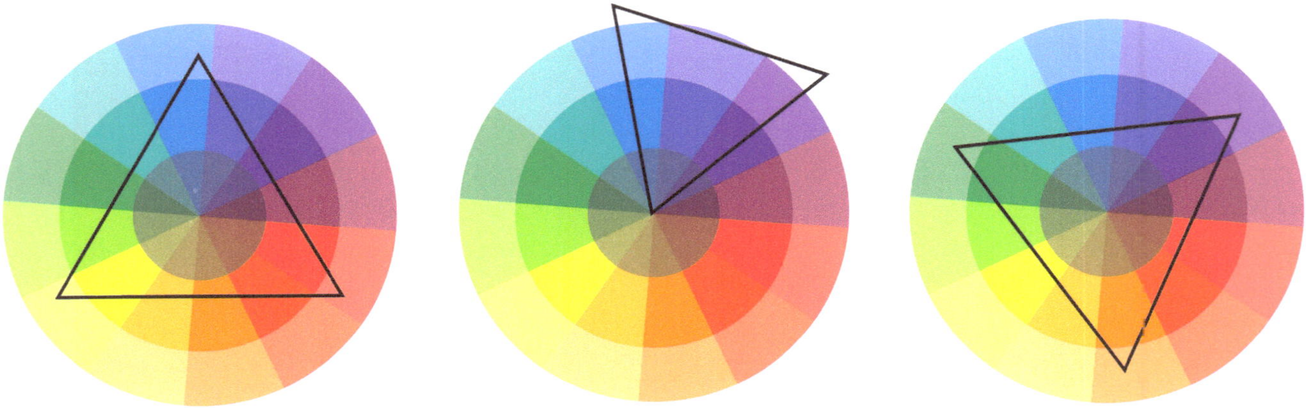

Color families that work well together also create harmony in a composition. Referring to the number three in terms of color, those color families which include three colors also tend to be more harmonious. If we take a look at a color wheel and superimpose a triangle on top, we can discover some great harmonies! Try twisting the triangle to play with the harmonies that can be created! And remember that using at least three values of one color will create more depth than only using one or two (notice also that our color wheel has three values of each color).

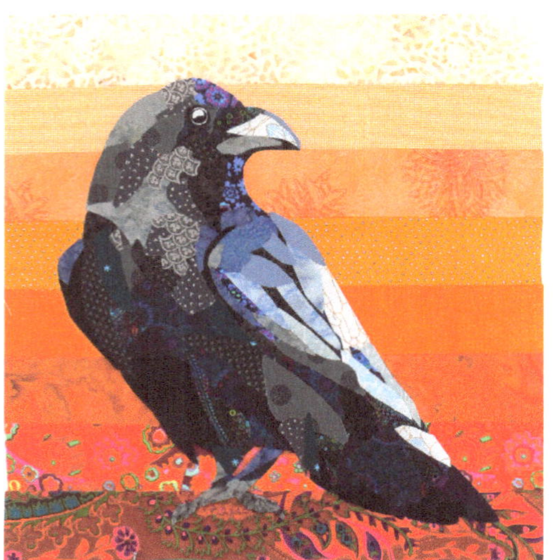

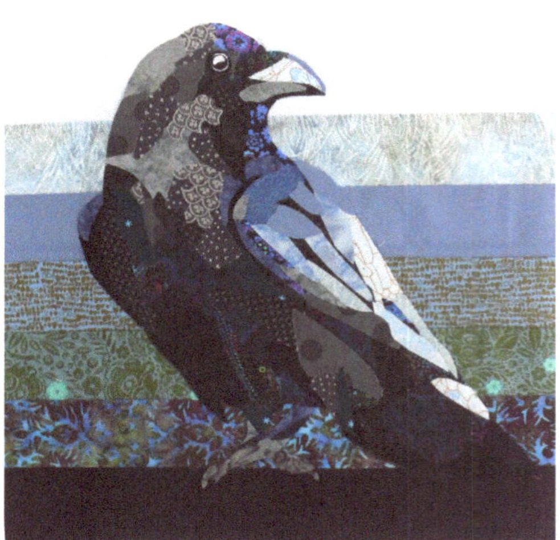

Both of these compositions are harmonious, but they feel very different from each other. The image on the left takes advantage of colors that are complementary from the blues in the bird. This color combination creates drama! The Raven on the right sits atop an analogous color palette which creates a more atmospheric and moody piece.

Balance is achieved when the composition is equally weighted from top to bottom and from side to side. It can also be in balance when the color palette is evenly distributed. This doesn't mean that the composition is symmetrical-- in fact, balance can be achieved with asymmetry.

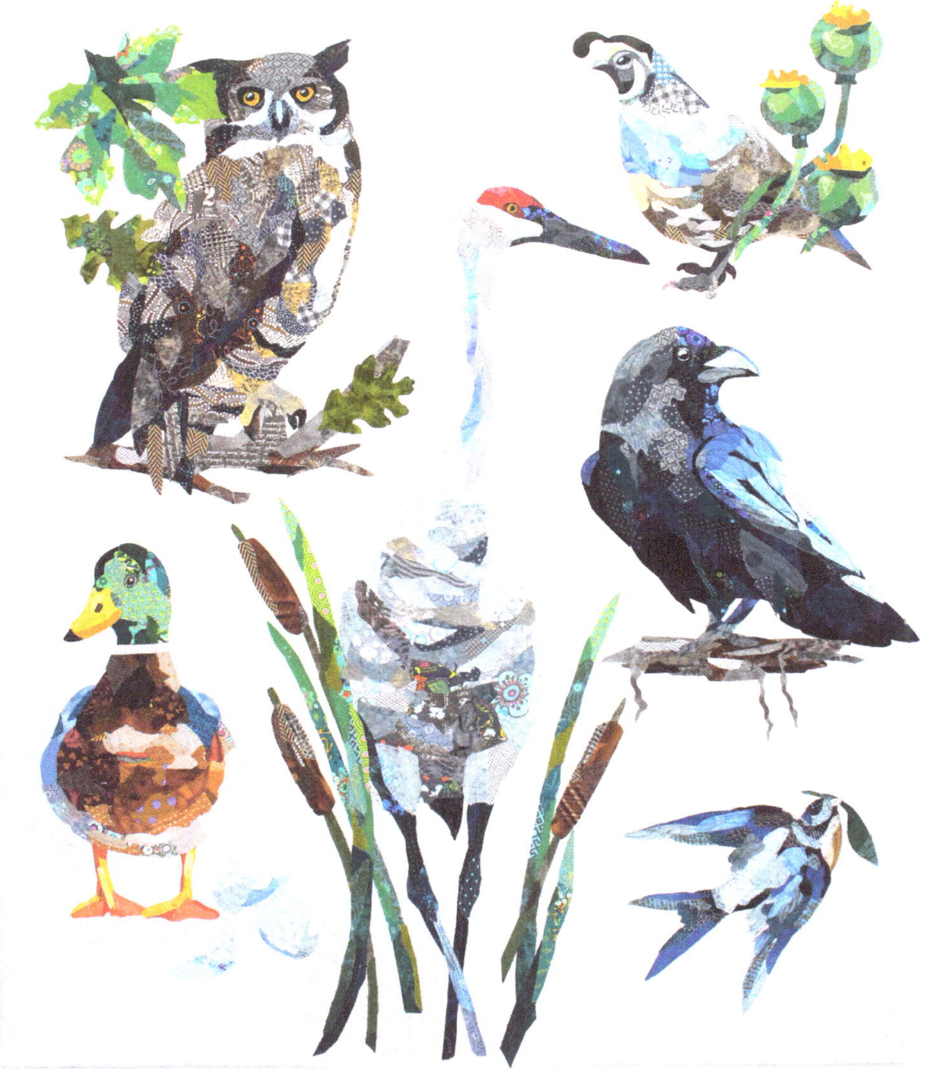

The heavy, dark Raven is balanced out by the lighter birds above and below him.

Likewise, the sizable Owl provides balance on the other side of the composition to the size and dark contrast of the Raven.

The weight of the grass and cattails in the lower center of the design is counterbalanced by the green leaves and flower pods in the upper corners.

The cool blue colors in the Quail, Raven, Swallow and Crane are balanced by the warm colors in the Duck and the Owl. Furthermore, the bright red crown of the Crane is balanced by the small touches of green in the composition.

SCALE

Scale refers to the spatial relationships between the elements and the negative space in the composition. The scale of each bird and the space between birds helps to establish *leading lines* that guide the eye around the composition.

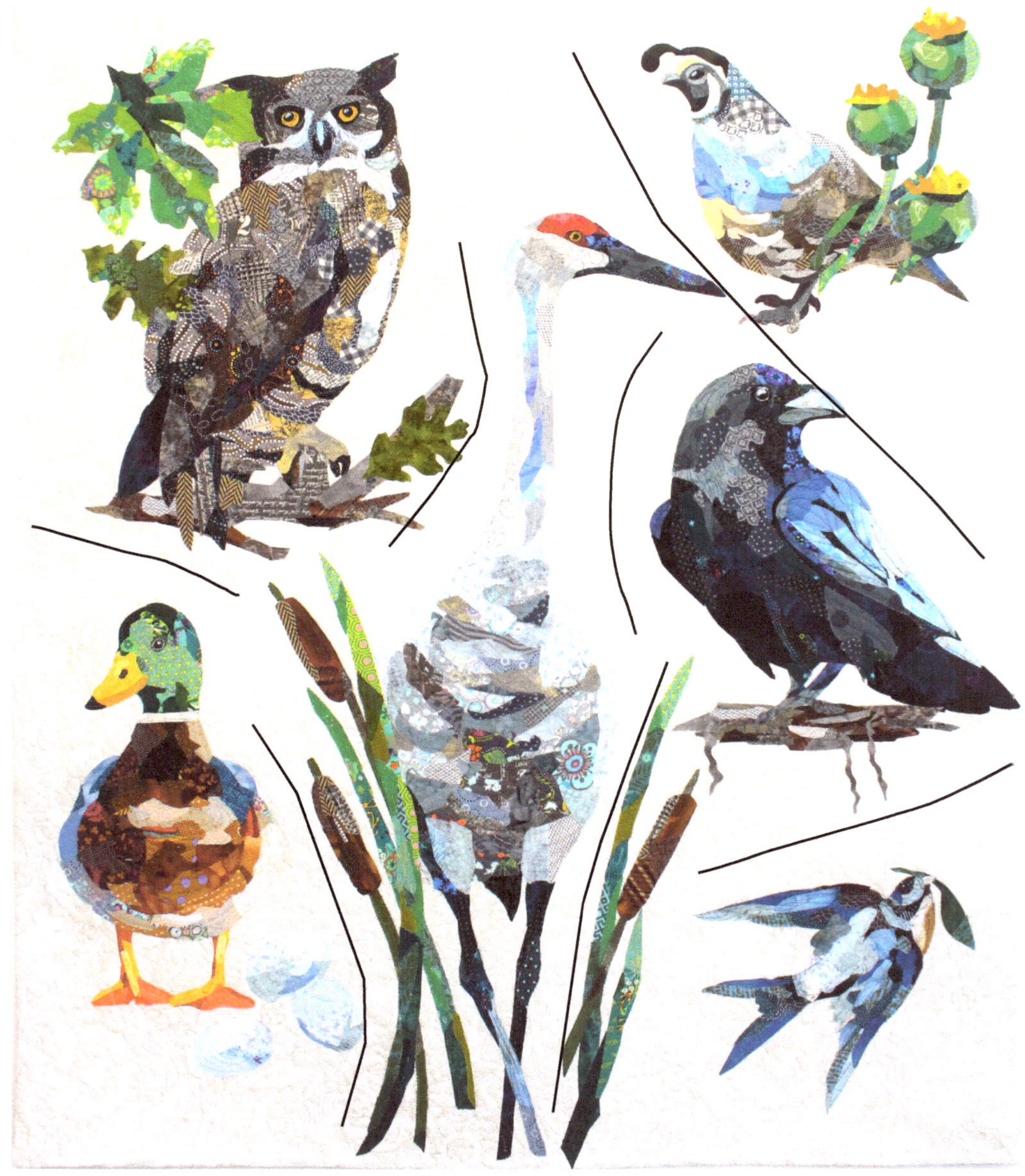

If I draw lines between the birds to emphasize the relationship between the shapes of the birds, it's easy to see the effect those shapes have on the movement of our eyes around the composition. When the distance between elements is too great, the leading lines dematerialize.

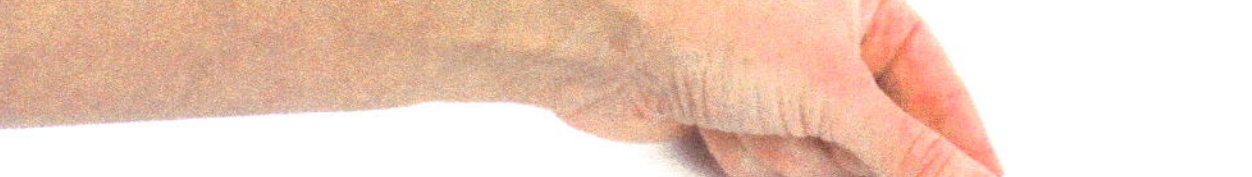

ART QUILT

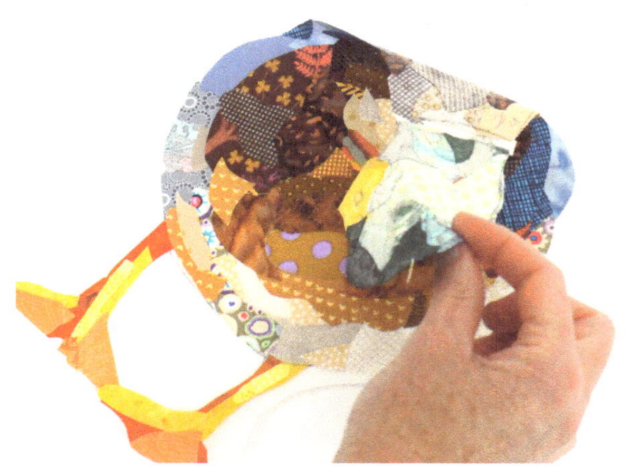

To create an art quilt that will hang on the wall, I will gently peel each piece away from the parchment paper and apply them to a background piece of fabric. The background can be solid (as mine is), or pieced.

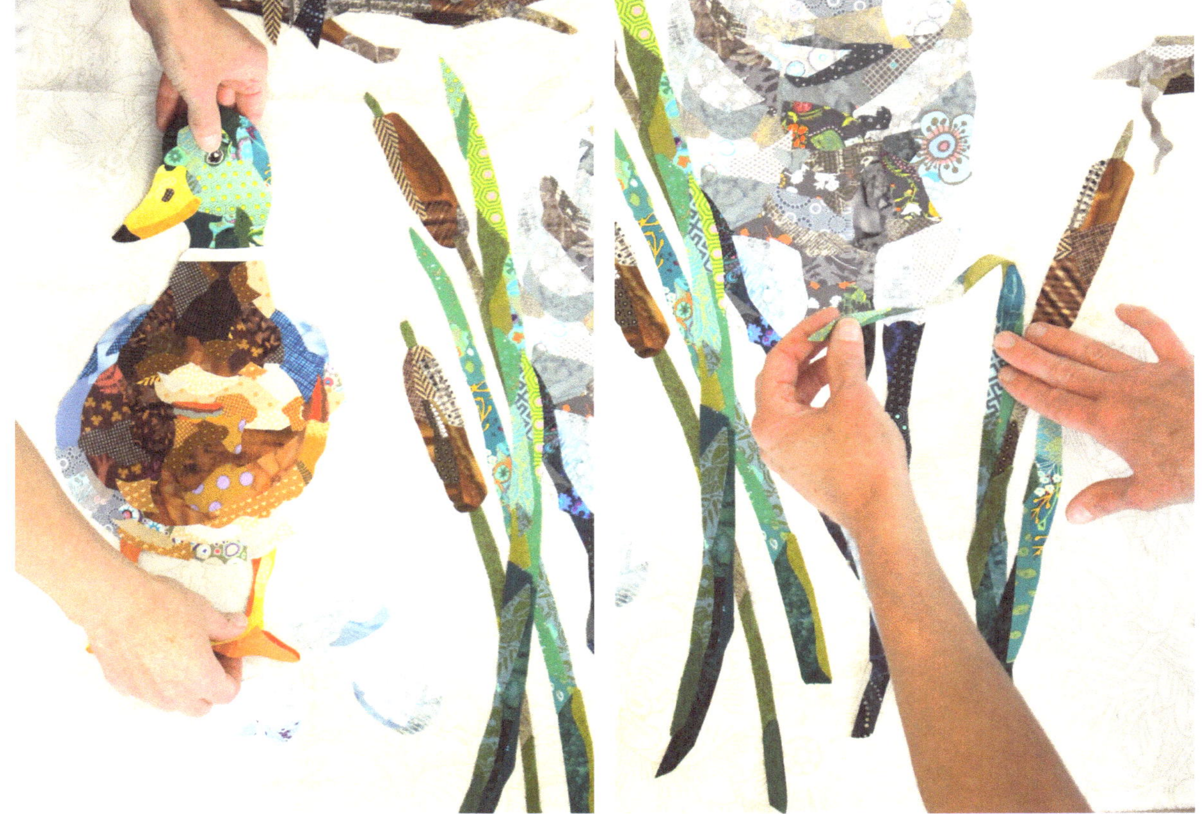

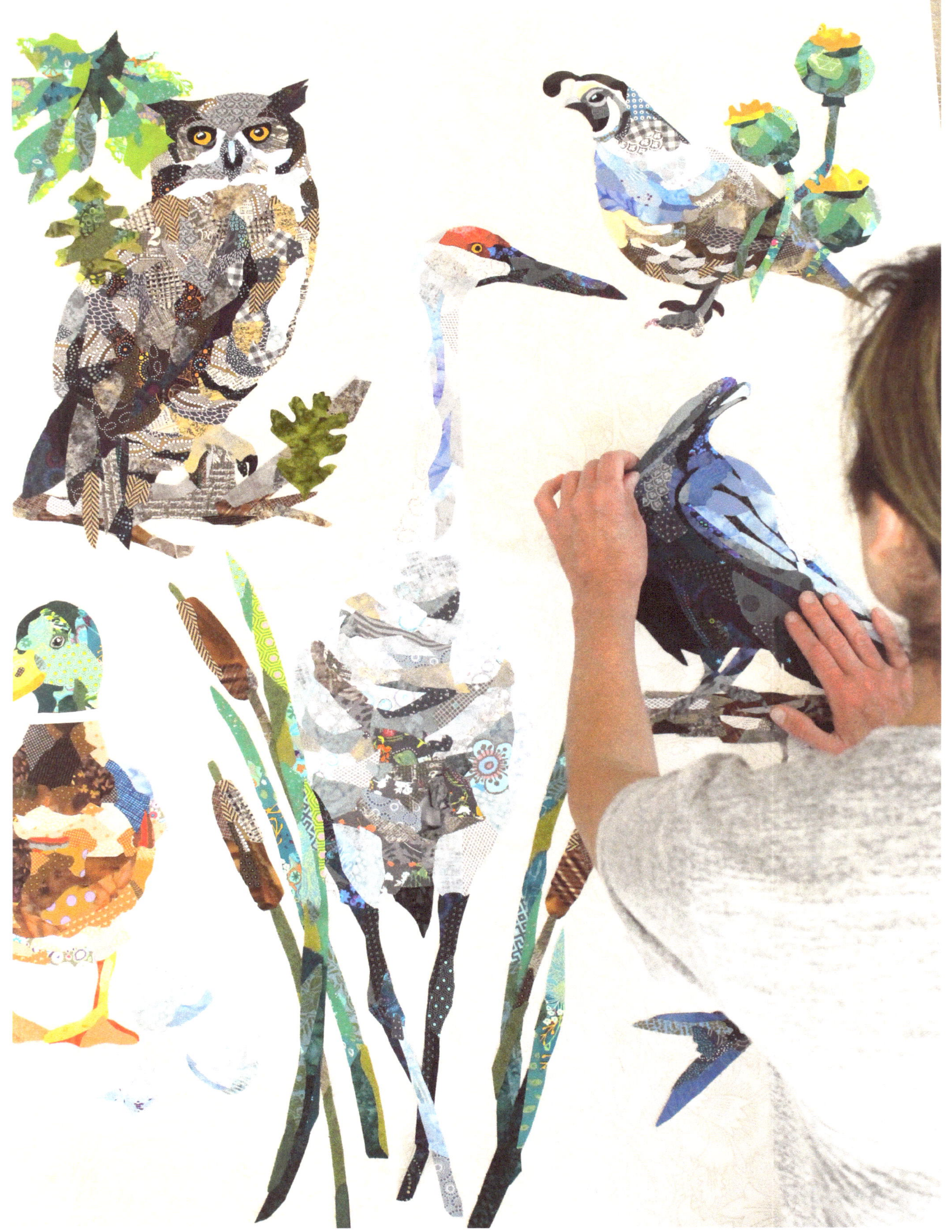

After applying each element and fussing with things until I'm satisfied, it's time to press!

Press with a hot, STEAMY iron to fuse the collaged elements to the background fabric. The steam from the iron will help the fabric to soften and make it easier to quilt through.

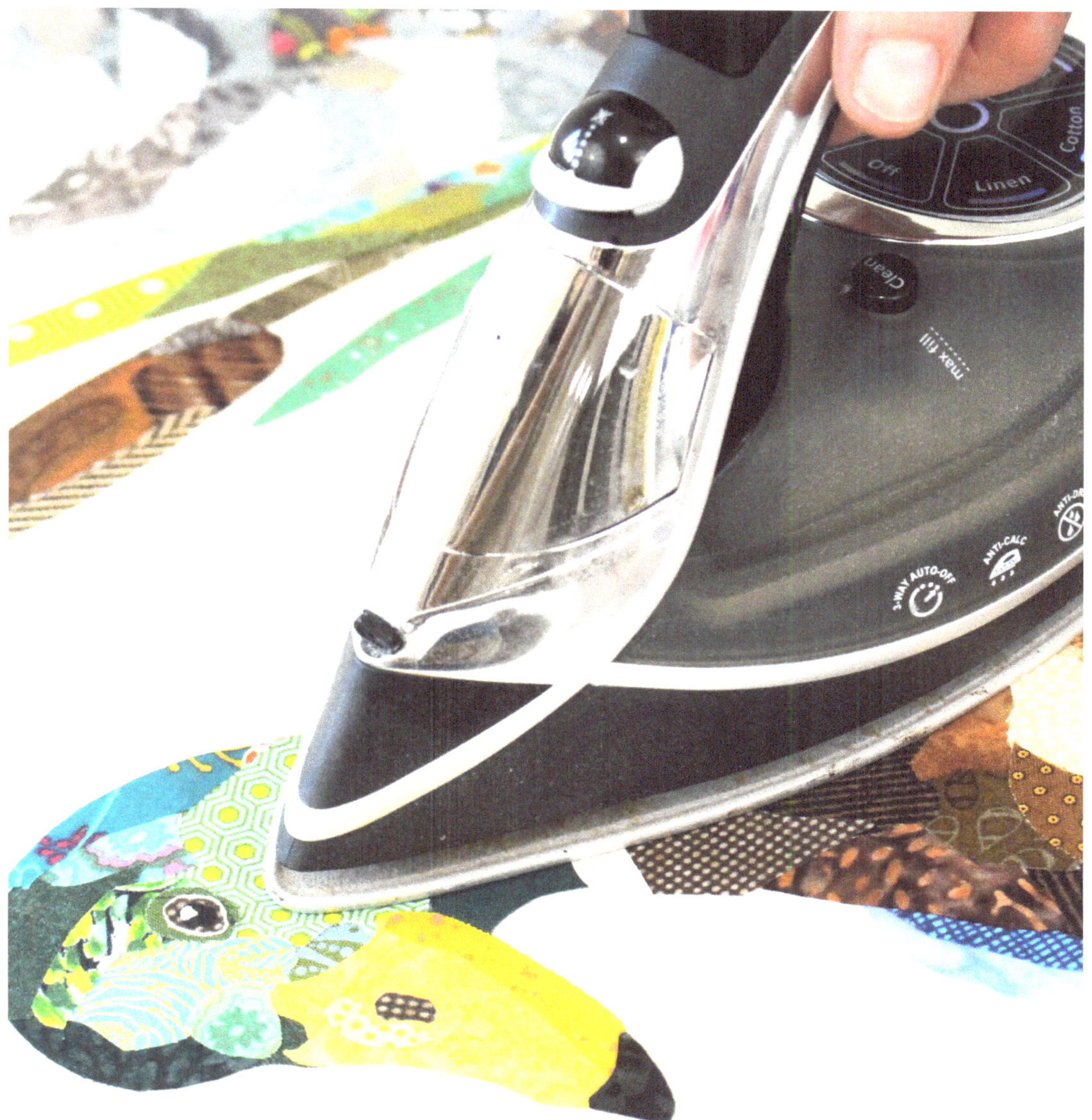

Did I mention that STEAM is key in this step?

Lite Steam a Seam 2 is designed to be pressed with steam. The steam will help to dissipate the temporary adhesive, and activate the permanent fusion of all the fabric pieces to each other and to the background.

<u>Quilting</u>

Because collage quilts are comprised of raw-edged pieces, I recommend dense quilting. However, it is not necessary to stitch around each piece! Following are the steps for completing the project as an art quilt.

One

Make a traditional "quilt sandwich", composed of backing, batting and the collaged quilt top.

Make certain that the backing and batting are about 4" larger than the quilt top around each edge. Pin the layers together with basting pins.

Use thin batting like Hobbs Thermore*.

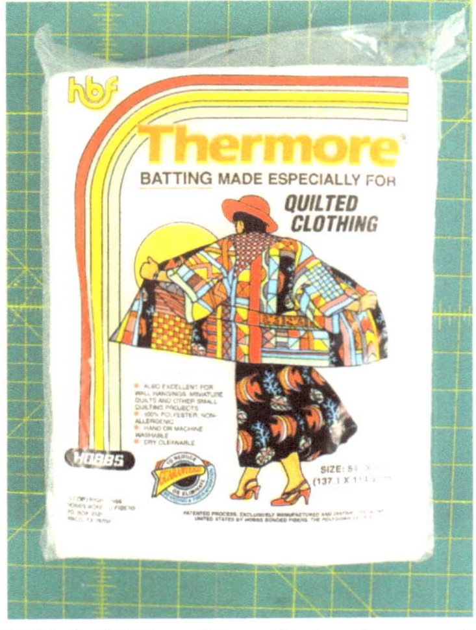

*This is NOT a paid product endorsement

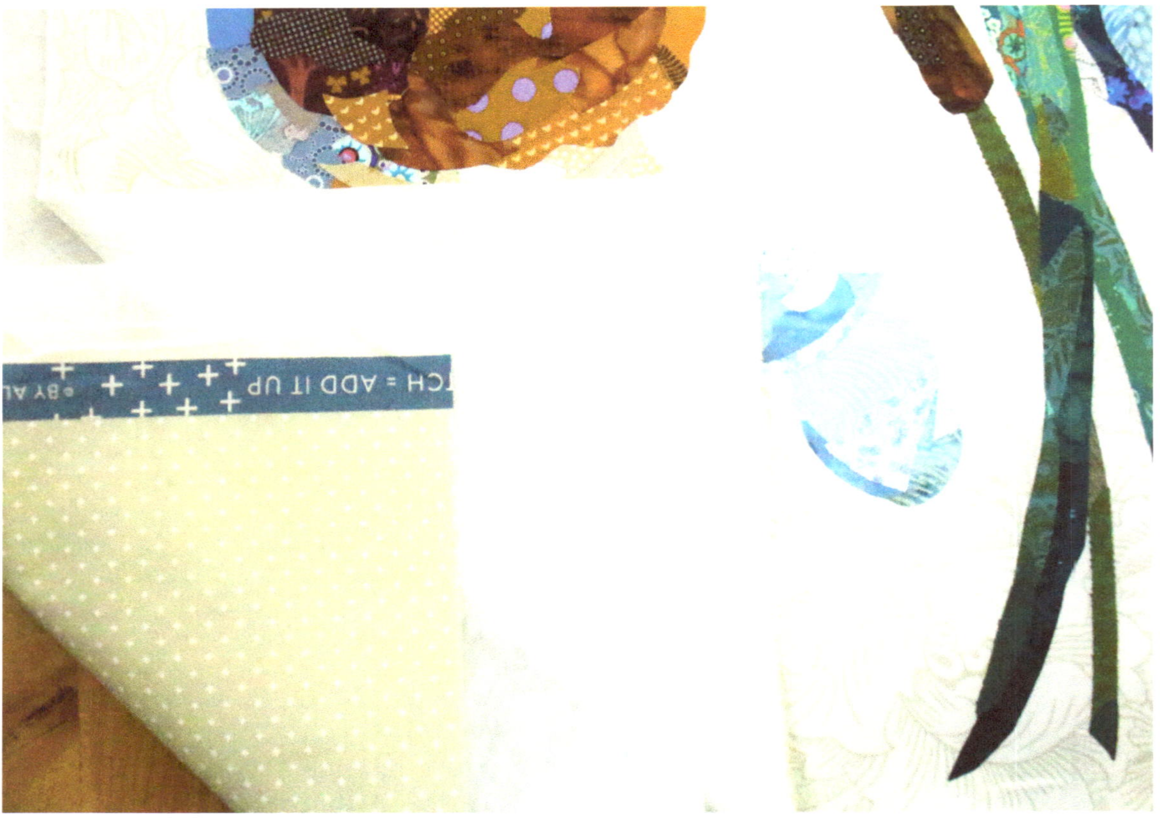

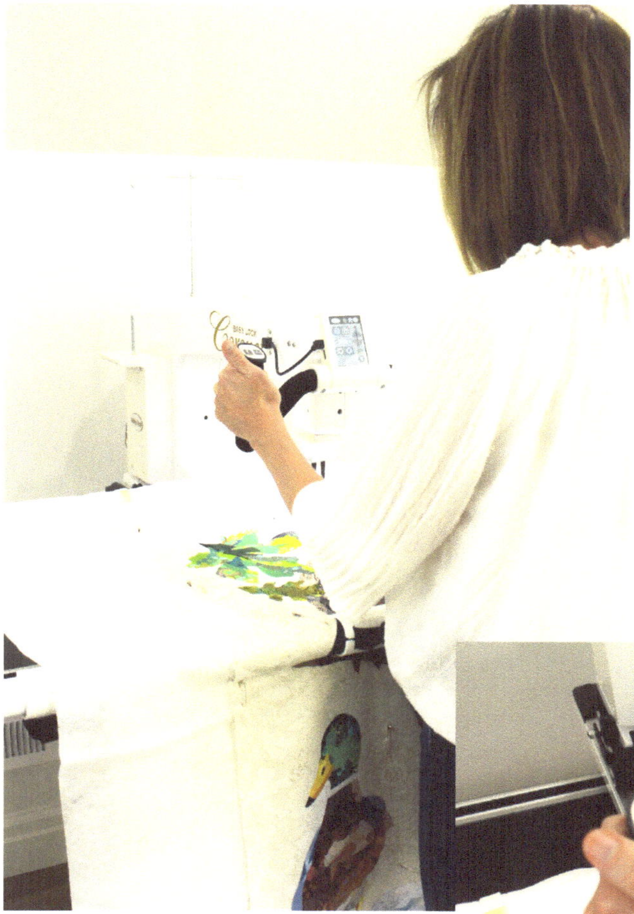

Two

Quilt the entire piece. Stitch lines should be no more than 1/2" apart to ensure that each piece is tacked down with stitching.

I quilted this project on my long-arm machine, but it can be quilted using a domestic machine as well. If using a domestic machine, I recommend using a stitch regulator foot that will allow you to do free-motion quilting. If your machine doesn't adapt to a stitch regulator, a walking foot is a good idea.

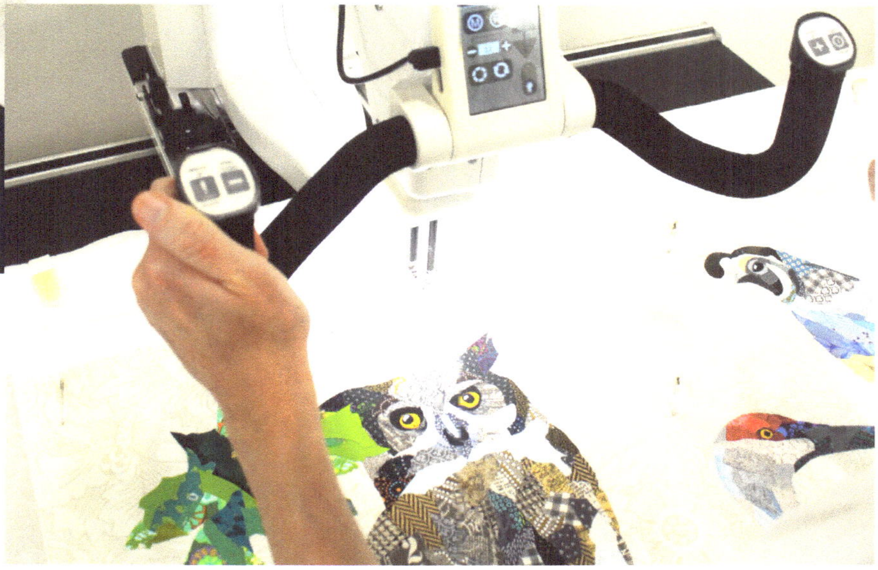

The thread I use is Superior Threads, Microquilter* #100 polyester thread. Polyester thread is stronger than cotton, and better suited for quilting through multiple fabric layers and fusible.

I selected neutral colors that blend into the quilt.

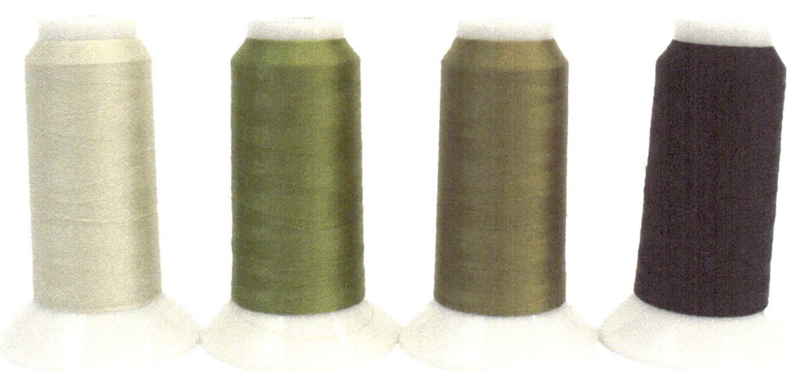

*This is NOT a paid product endorsement

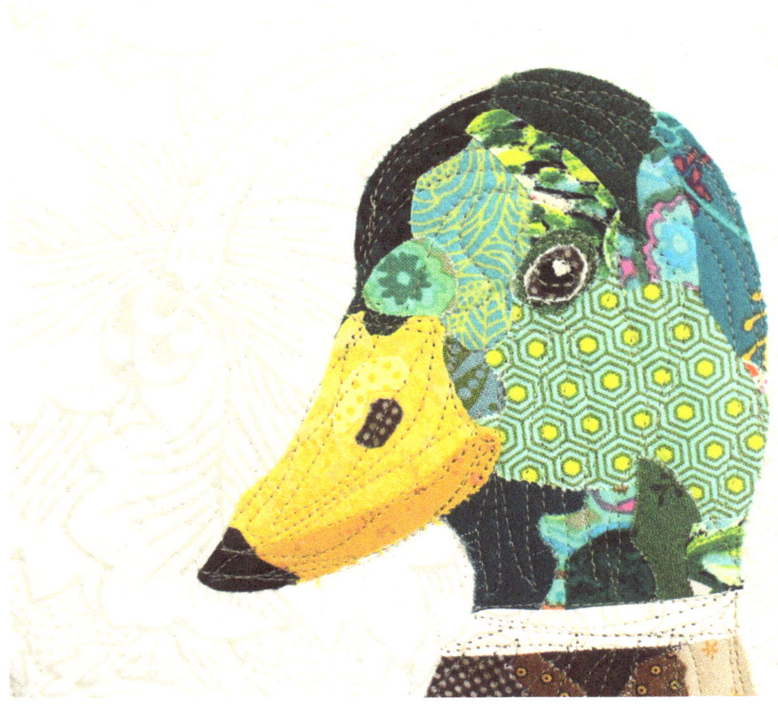

The background quilting design of my quilt is an allover meandering stipple, while the quilting on each of the birds is "doodle-stitching". The quilting blends into the design when using microquilter thread, and that's how I want it because I'm not a great quilter. Furthermore, I want the focus to be on the collage, not the quilting!

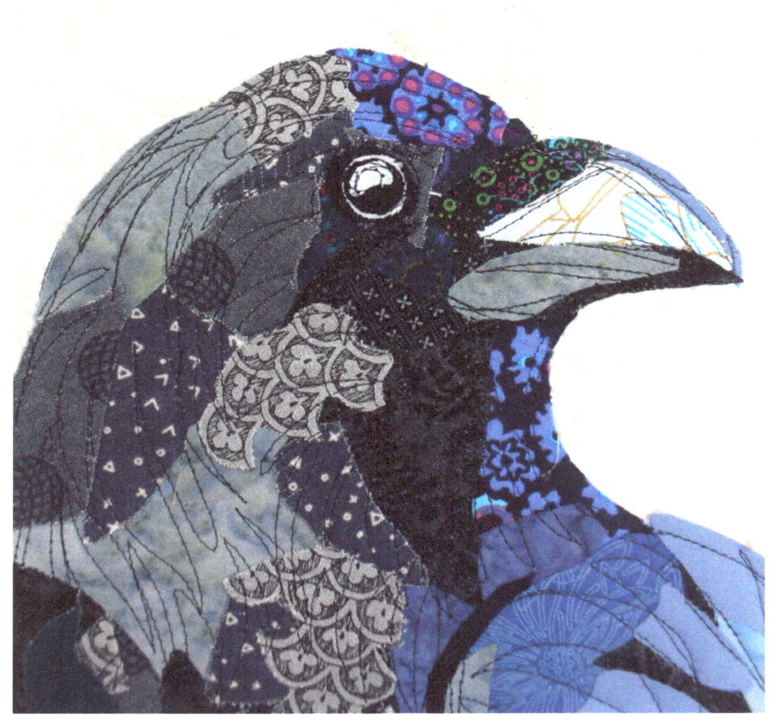

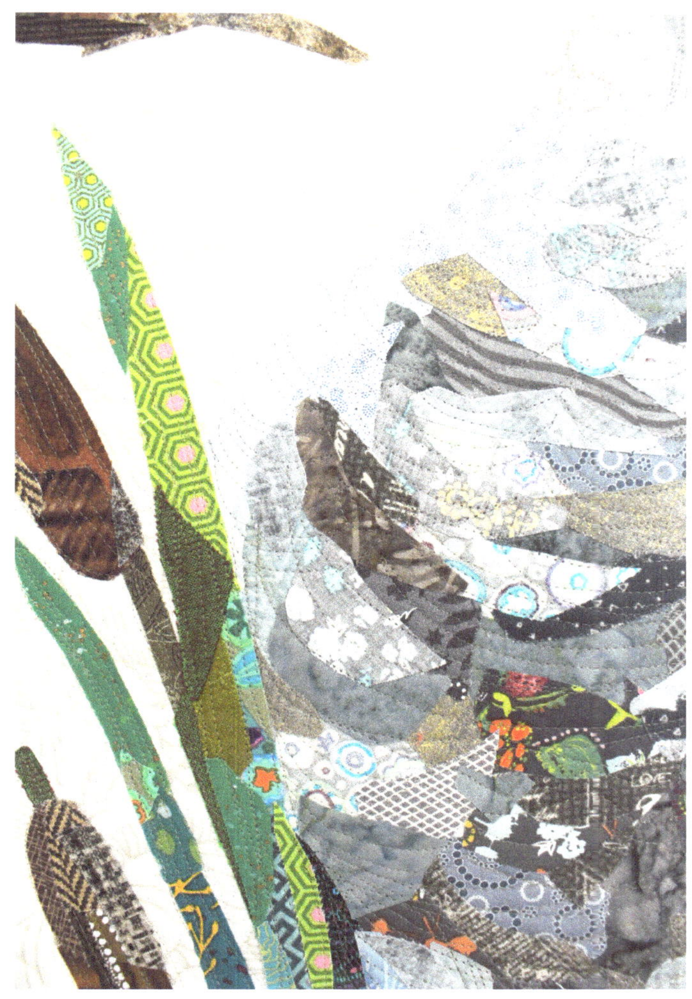

Common Quilting Questions

Should I use a special needle when quilting?

Always be sure to use a sharp needle! Titanium needles are especially good for collage quilts because they resist breaking and bending. Also, non-stick needles (designed with an anti-adhesive or Teflon coating) are perfect for quilting a collage quilt.

How can I avoid getting residue from fusible on my needle?

The use of a non-stick needle will minimize residue on the needle of your machine. But to clean any residue that does accumulate, simply wipe the needle with a cotton ball saturated in rubbing alcohol.

Can I wash a collage quilt?

Generally, a collage quilt is considered an art quilt, and not used as a bed quilt. However, if you keep in mind that the raw-edged pieces used in the quilt will fray (and plan accordingly) there is nothing stopping you from washing the quilt. The key to ensure that a collage quilt washes up nicely is dense quilting so that each piece is secured to the foundation fabric. When in doubt, test it out by making a small sample and running it through the wash on delicate cycle.

Three

Square up the quilt~ (Measure and trim the edges to ensure that the corners are right angles and each edge is straight).

Finish the raw edges of the quilt by binding or applying a facing.

Facing a Quilt

Facing is an easy way to finish a quilt and has a clean, modern look.

To add facing, cut 4 strips of fabric that are 3" - 4" by the length of each side of the quilt. Fold and press the strips in half with wrong sides together to create strips that are the length of each side of the quilt. Also, cut four 5" squares. Fold and press the squares in half with wrong sides together to create triangles.

Line the raw edges of the triangles up with the corners on the front of the quilt.

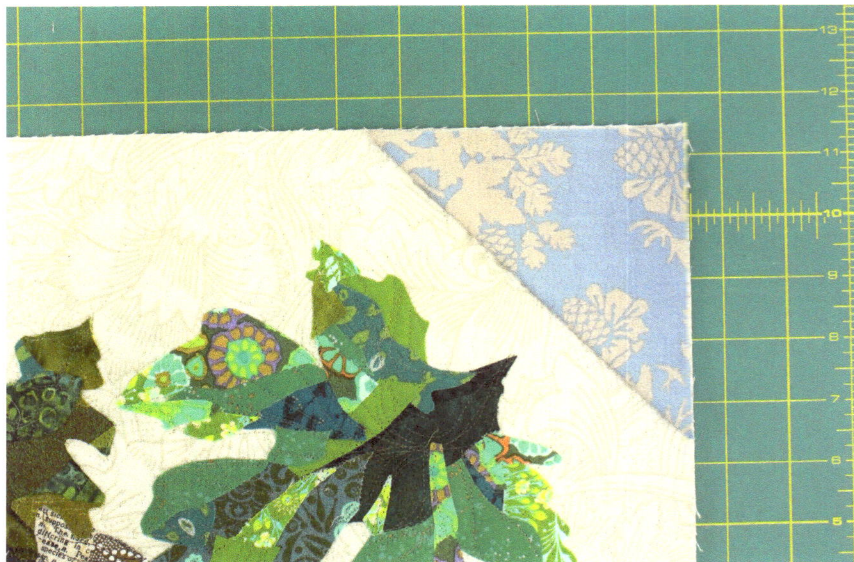

Line the strips up with the raw edges of the quilt as well (on top of the corner triangles). Trim the strips to measure approximately half-way along the edge of the triangles.

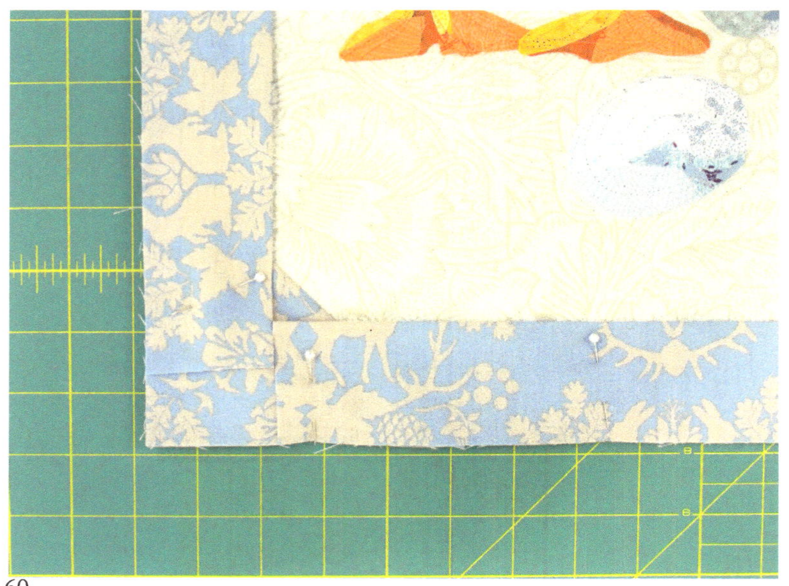

Stitch along the edges of the quilt with a 1/4" seam. Run the stitch off the edges, and backstitch to ensure the corners are secure.

I am using a walking foot on my machine, which is helpful when sewing through multiple layers.

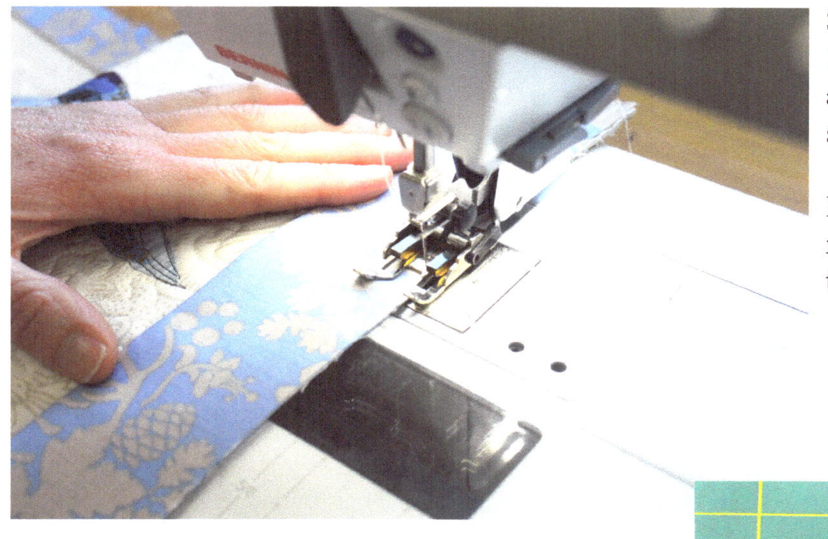

Trim the corners to reduce bulk and press the strips away from the quilt.

Turn the corners and facing strips to the back side of the quilt. Press in place with a hot, steamy iron and hand stitch or use fusible web to secure the facing strips to the back of the quilt.

The open corner pockets are perfect for inserting a dowel to hang the quilt!

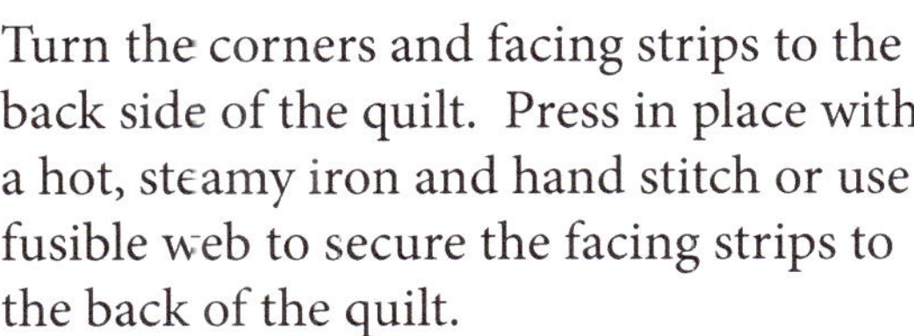

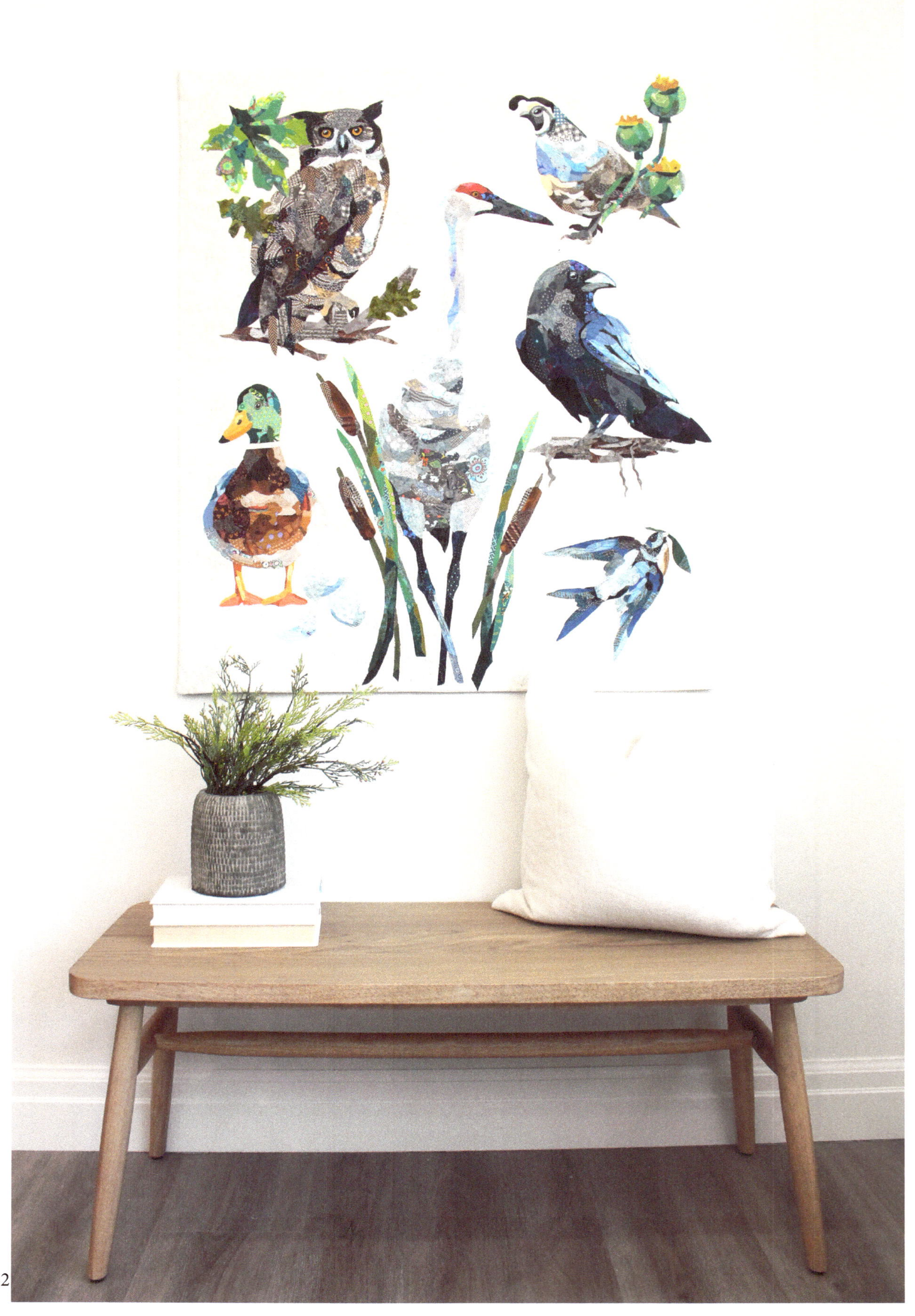

It's easy to use one of the birds to make a small piece of artwork! A touch of embroidery on the project makes it especially whimsical and special.

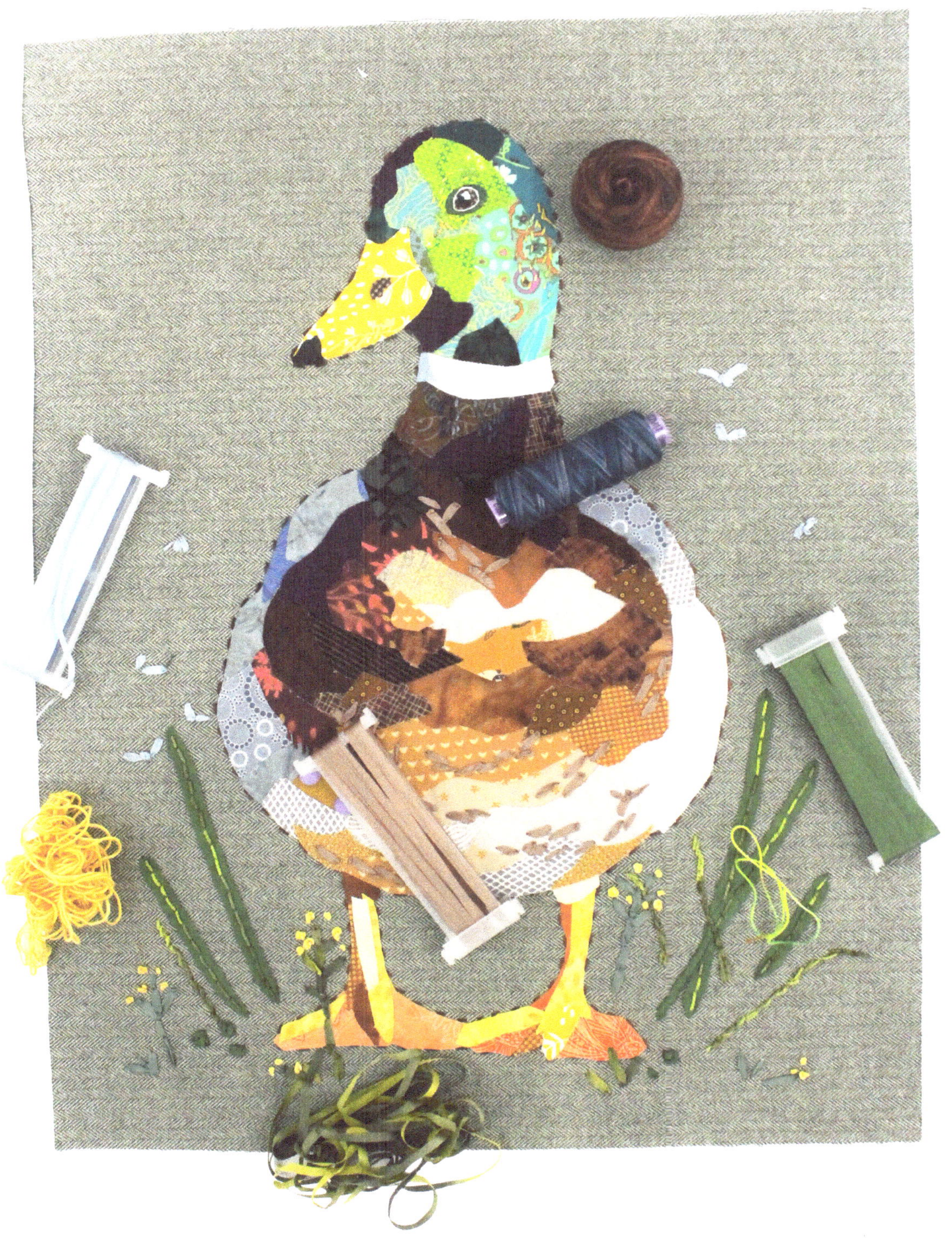

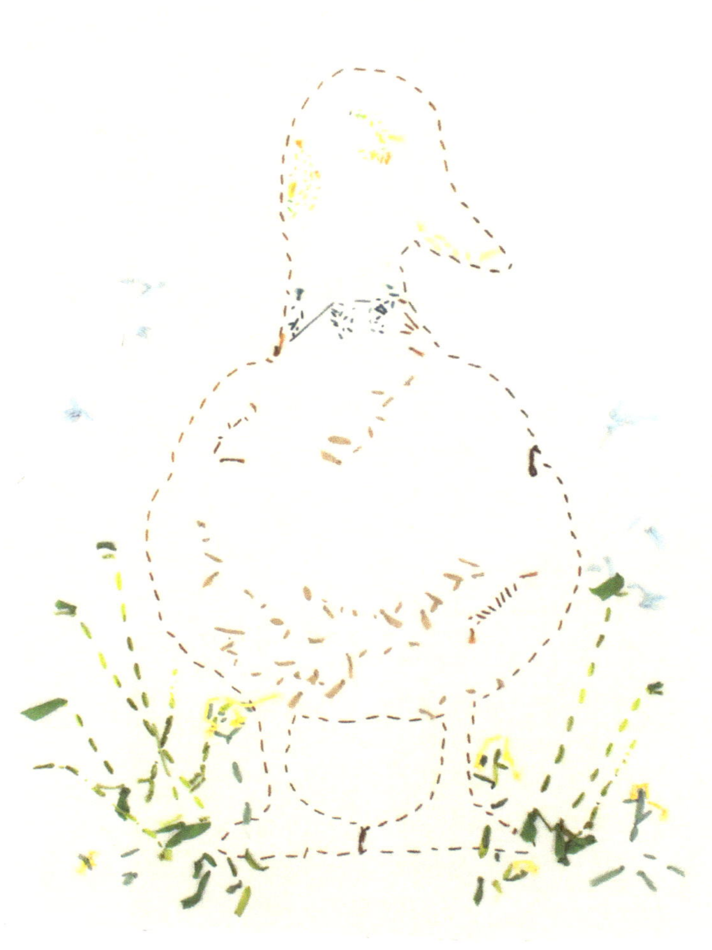

I apply Pellon Shape-Flex All Purpose Fusible Interfacing to the back side of the finished collage piece. This adds stability to the fabric while I embroider it.

I embroider using a variety of silk embroidery ribbon and Perle #5 thread. I'm especially partial to the Sue Spargo collection of Eleganza WonderFil Thread.*

*NOT a paid product endorsement

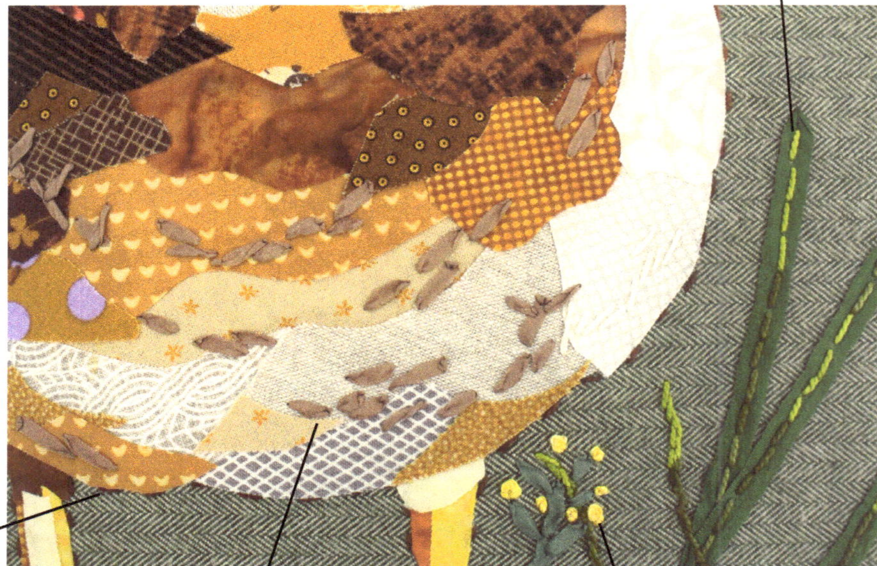

The stitches that I use are very simple (and quite sloppy).

To begin stitching with silk ribbon, "lock" the ribbon with your needle by piercing the end of it and pulling on the reverse end.

Silk ribbon will fray and run if pulled through fabric too many times, so cut the ribbon in increments of about 12" long.

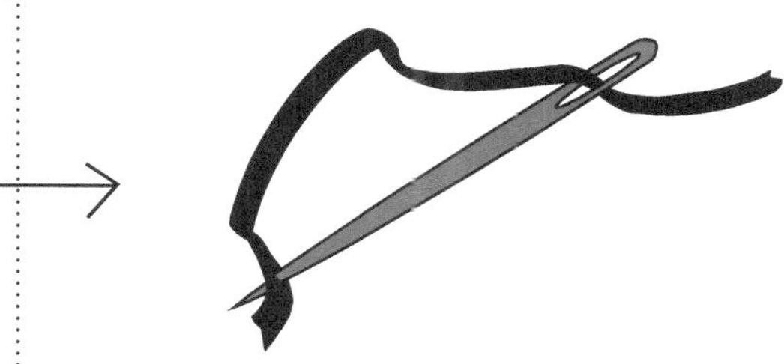

Stitch No. 1 Running Stitch

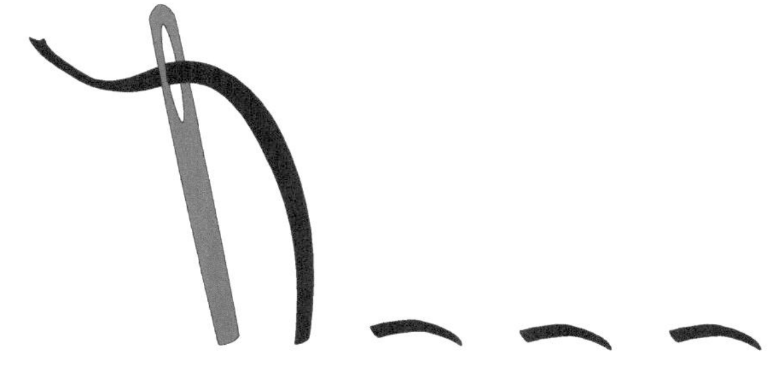

Stitch No. 2 Back Stitch

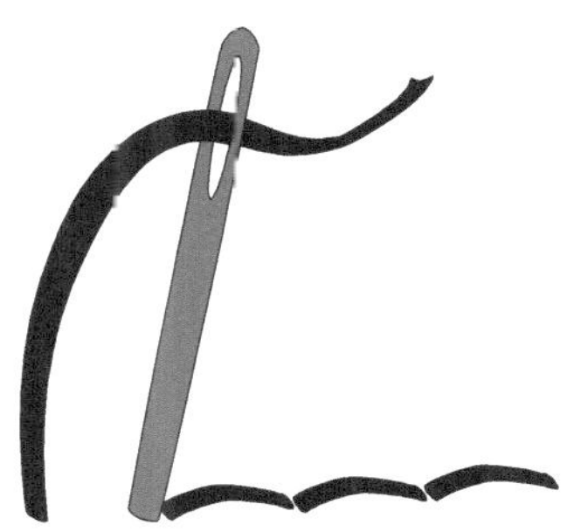

Stitch No. 3 French Knot

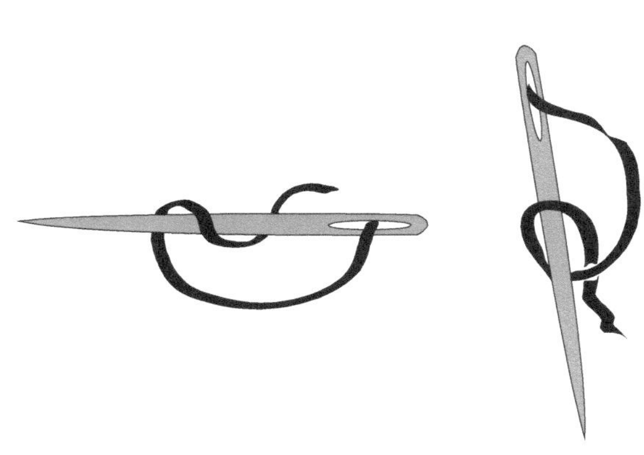

Stitch No. 4 Ribbon Stitch

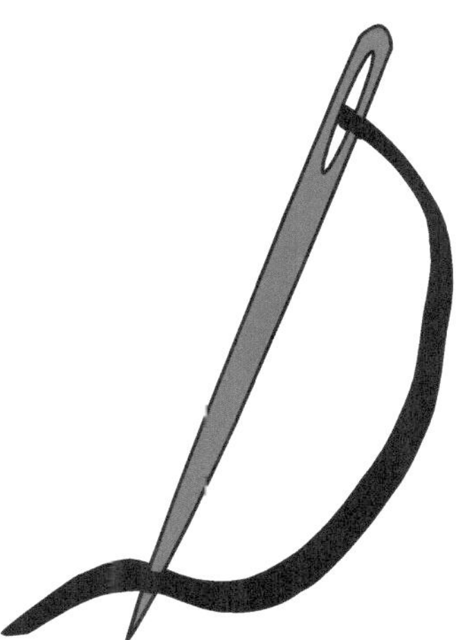

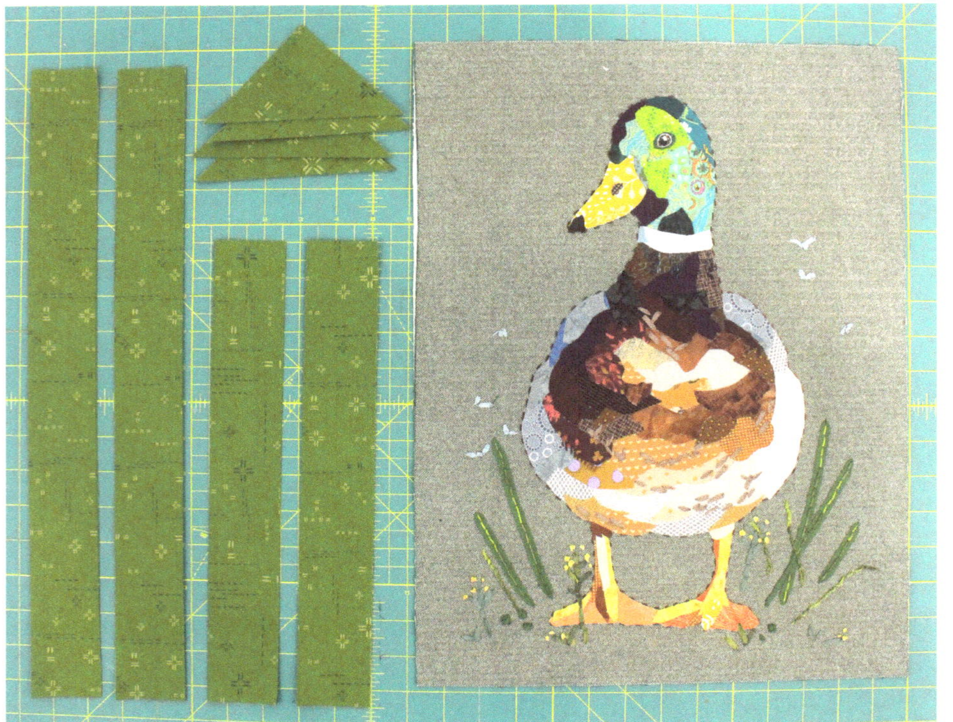

When I am finished adding some embroidery highlights to the duck, I add facing to complete the project.

You do not need to finish the edges if you choose to frame the artwork. However, since I decide to use a poster hanger, I want the edges finished.

The corner pockets of the facing are perfect for holding the hanger!

The poster hanger that I used for this project can be found on Amazon.com. Scan this code for the link!

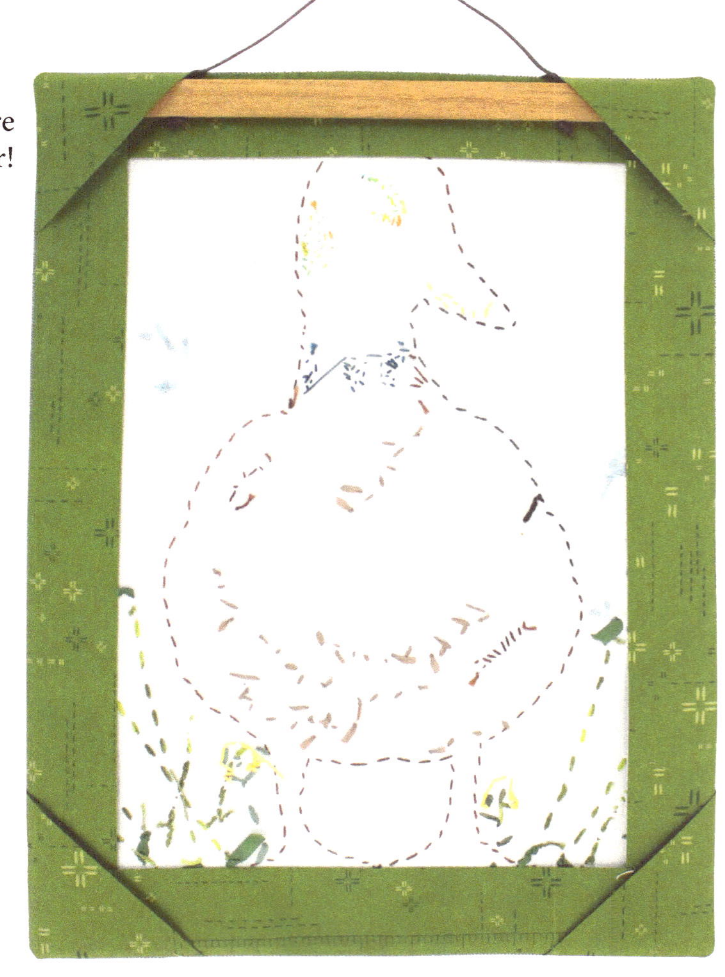

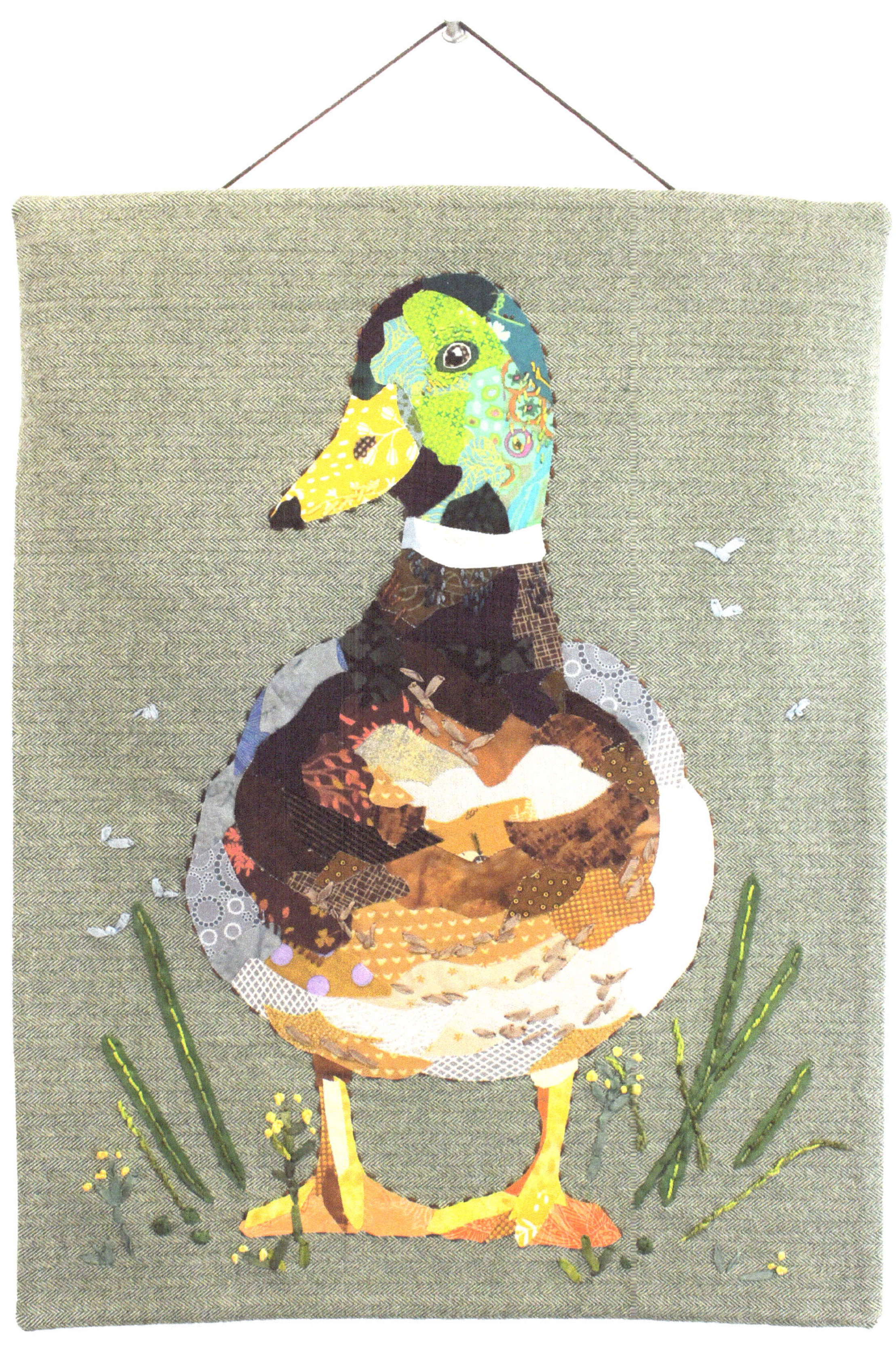

DECORATIVE PILLOW

Another way to use the textile collage is to make a decorative pillow cover, as I did with this Raven. Here are the step for making a pillow...

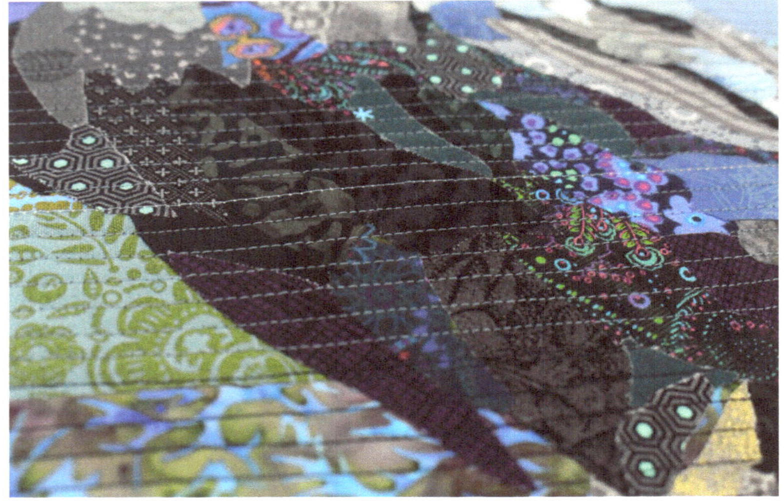

I quilted my pillow top with horizontal lines that are 1/4" apart. The lines mimic the pieced background and further make the raven blend with the background.

One Measure the pillow insert to cover. Adhere the finished collage to background fabric that is a few inches larger that the size of the pillow insert. (Background can be solid or pieced). Quilt if desired. Trim the complete mini quilt to the size of the pillow insert.

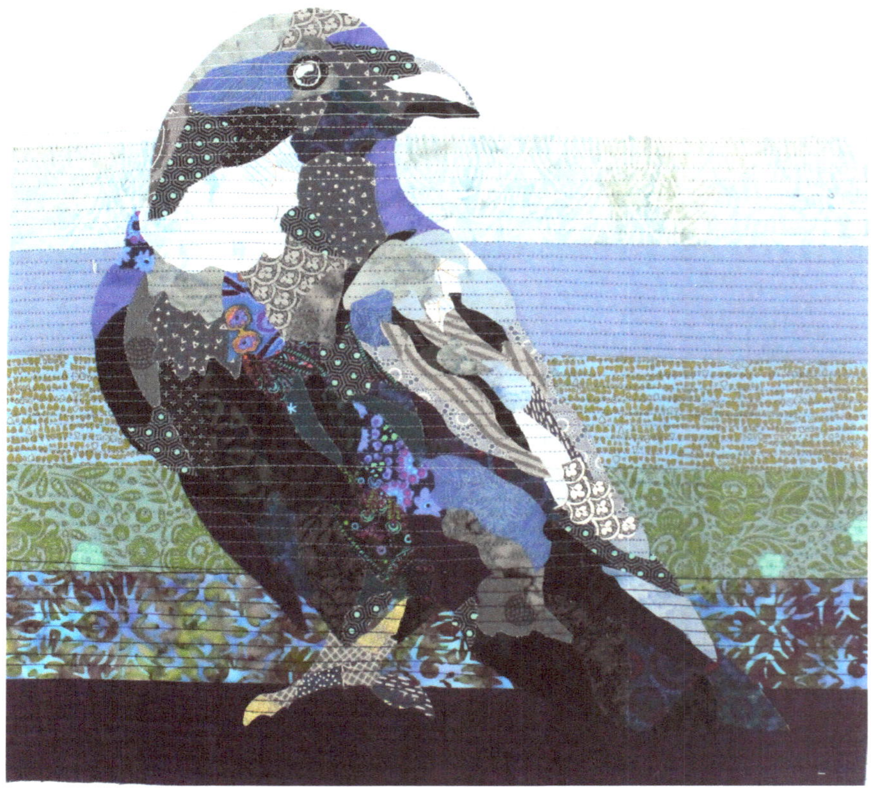

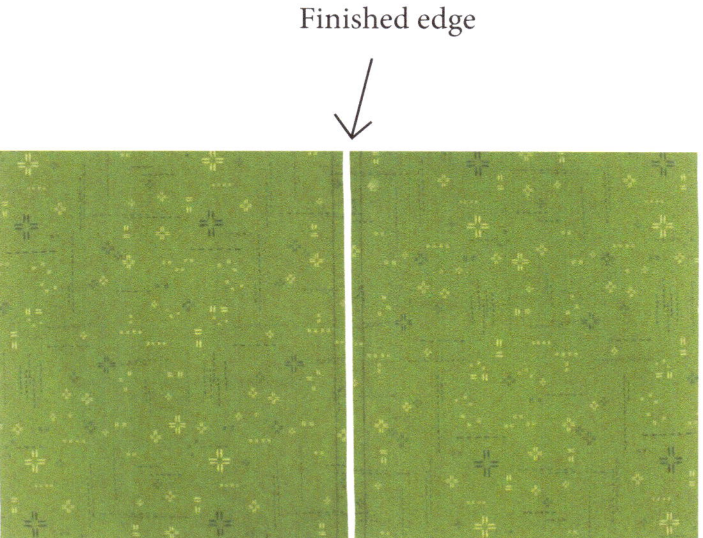

For my 15" square pillow insert, the back fabric for
the pillow measures 15" x 23". After cutting in half,
each piece measures 15" x 11.5".

TWO Cut fabric for the back of the pillow that is the same width of the pillow insert by the height + 6" - 8" (width x height + 6"). Cut that fabric piece in half, creating two rectangular pieces of fabric. Fold and stitch along one of the long edges to finish the raw edge.

Three Overlap the two back pieces and line them up with the edges of the front of the pillow, right sides together. Make certain that the opening for the pillow is horizontal with the top of the pillow. With a 1/2" seam, sew around the edges.

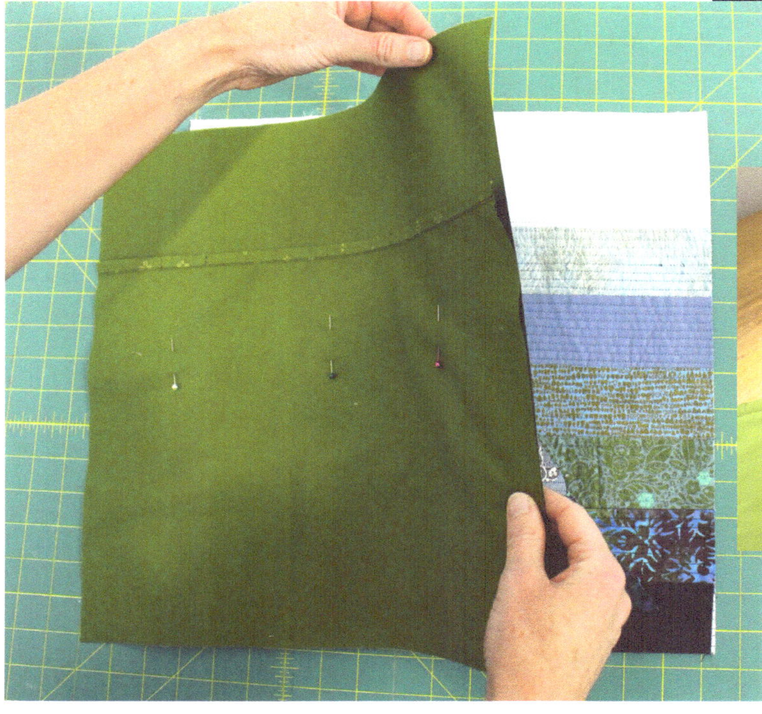

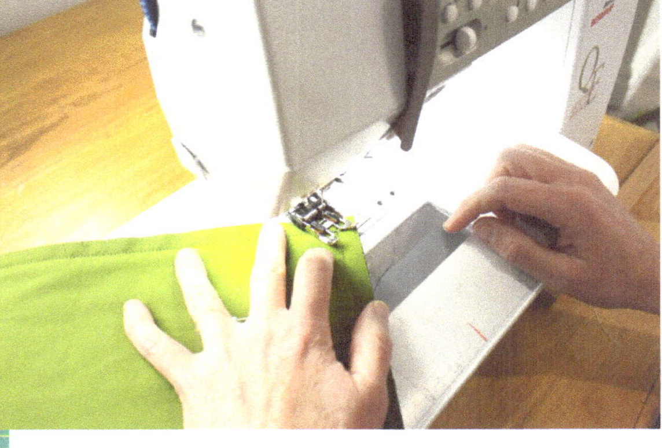

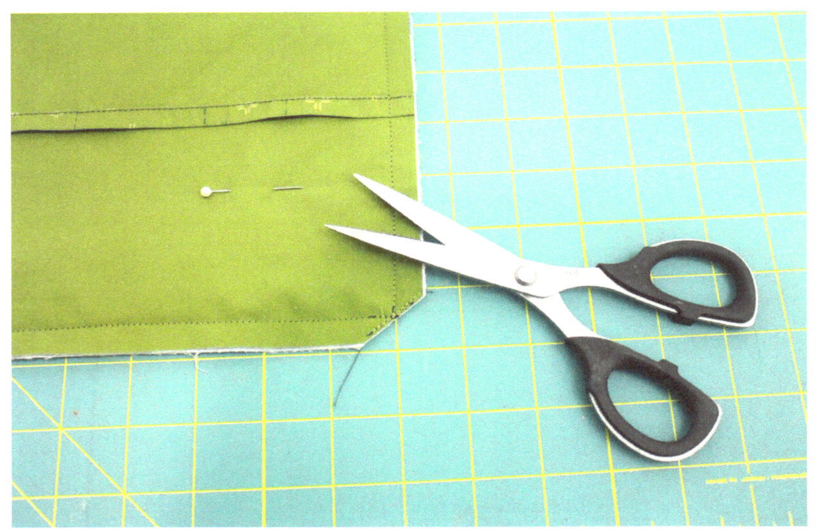

Four Stitch a diagonal line across the corners to reinforce them, then trim the corners to reduce bulk. Turn the pillow inside out through the back opening.

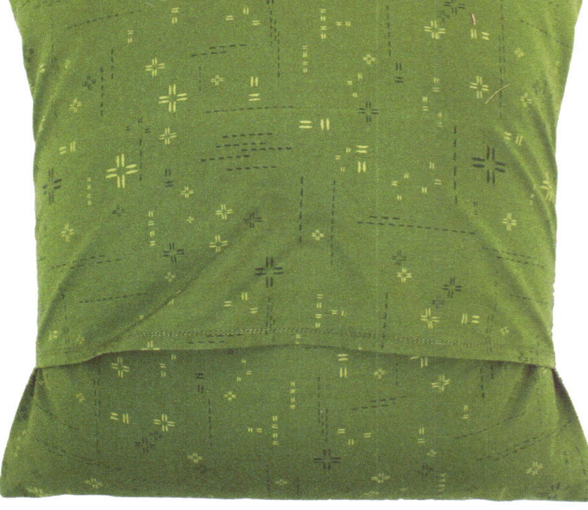

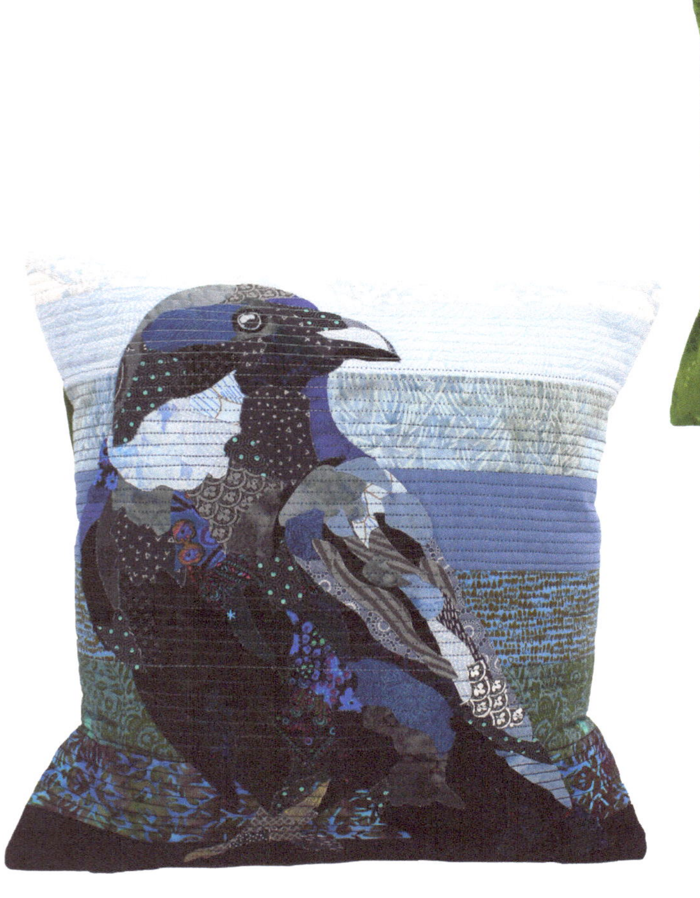

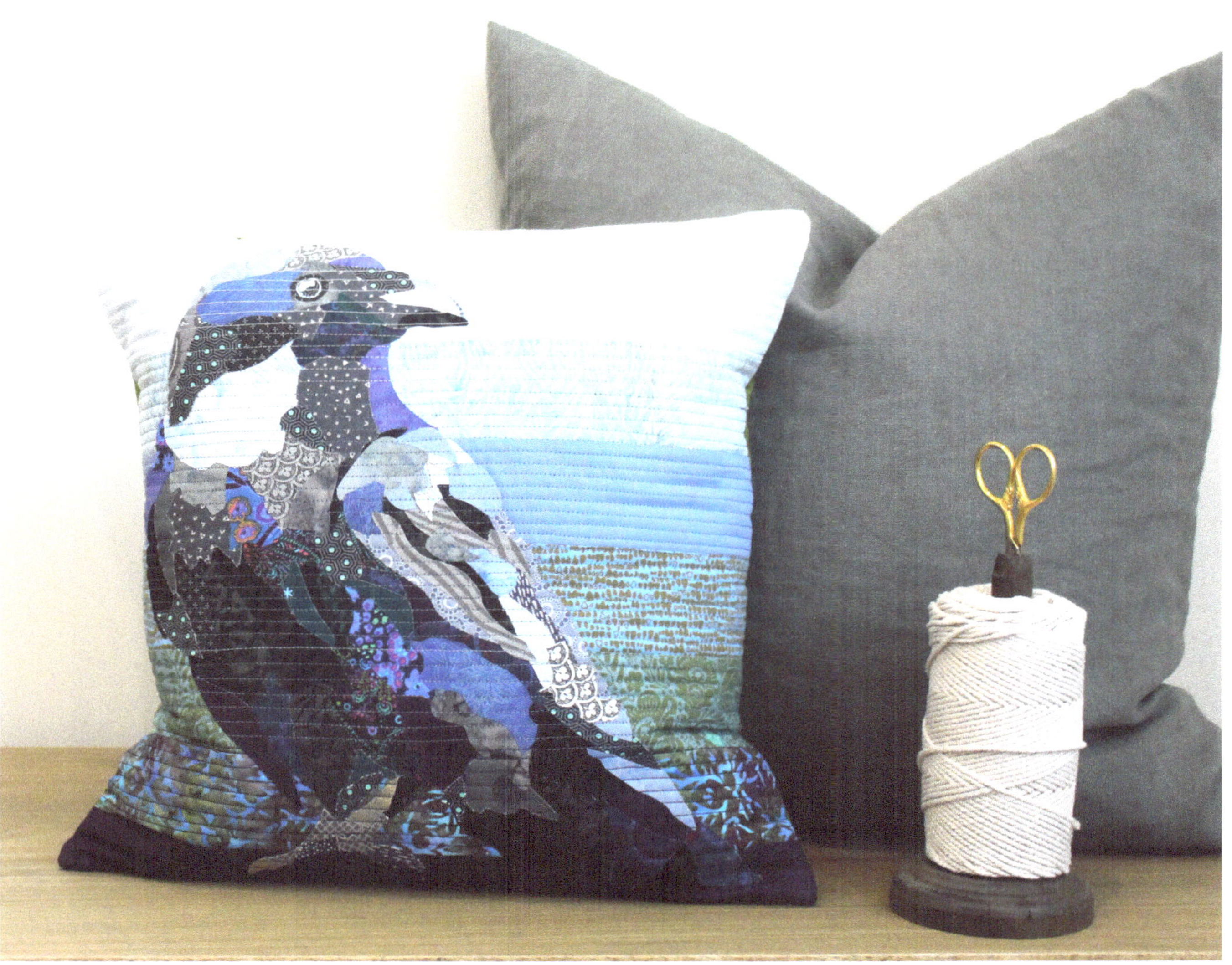

Thank you for joining me on this creative journey into textile collage! I hope you enjoy the projects from this book and that you'll share your work with me on social media.

Best of luck!

~Emily

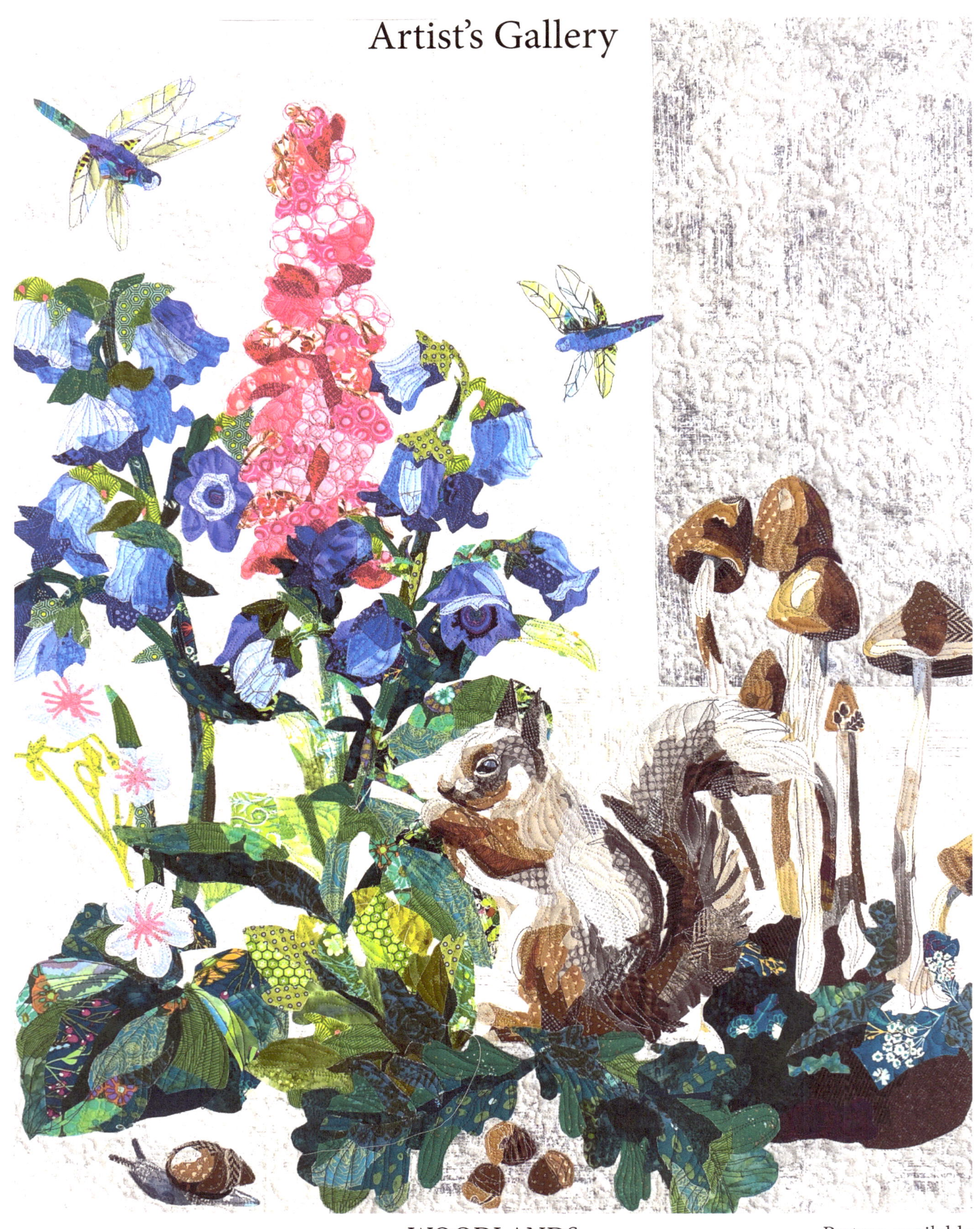

WOODLANDS
26" x 32"

Pattern available

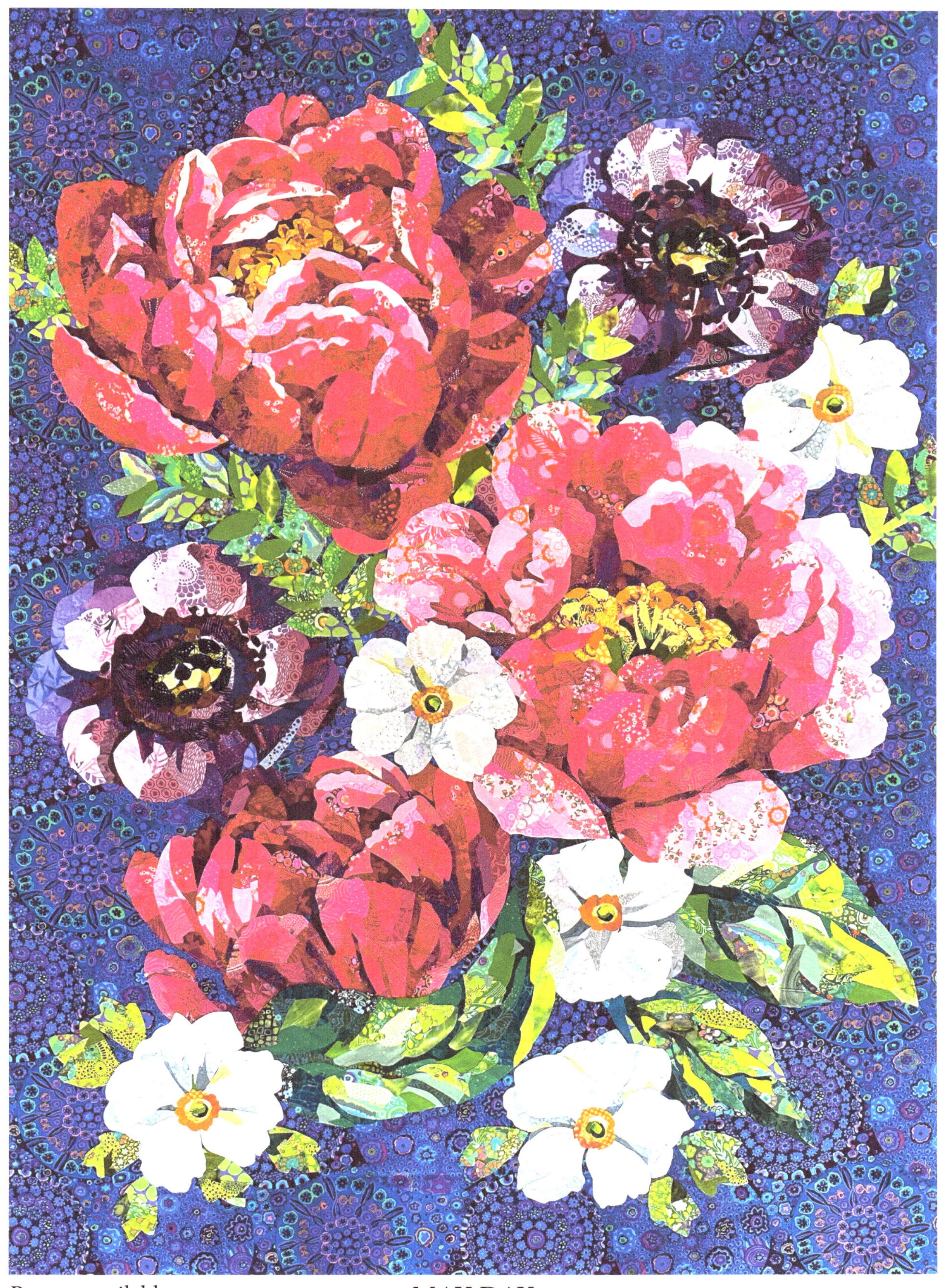

MAY DAY
43" X 60"

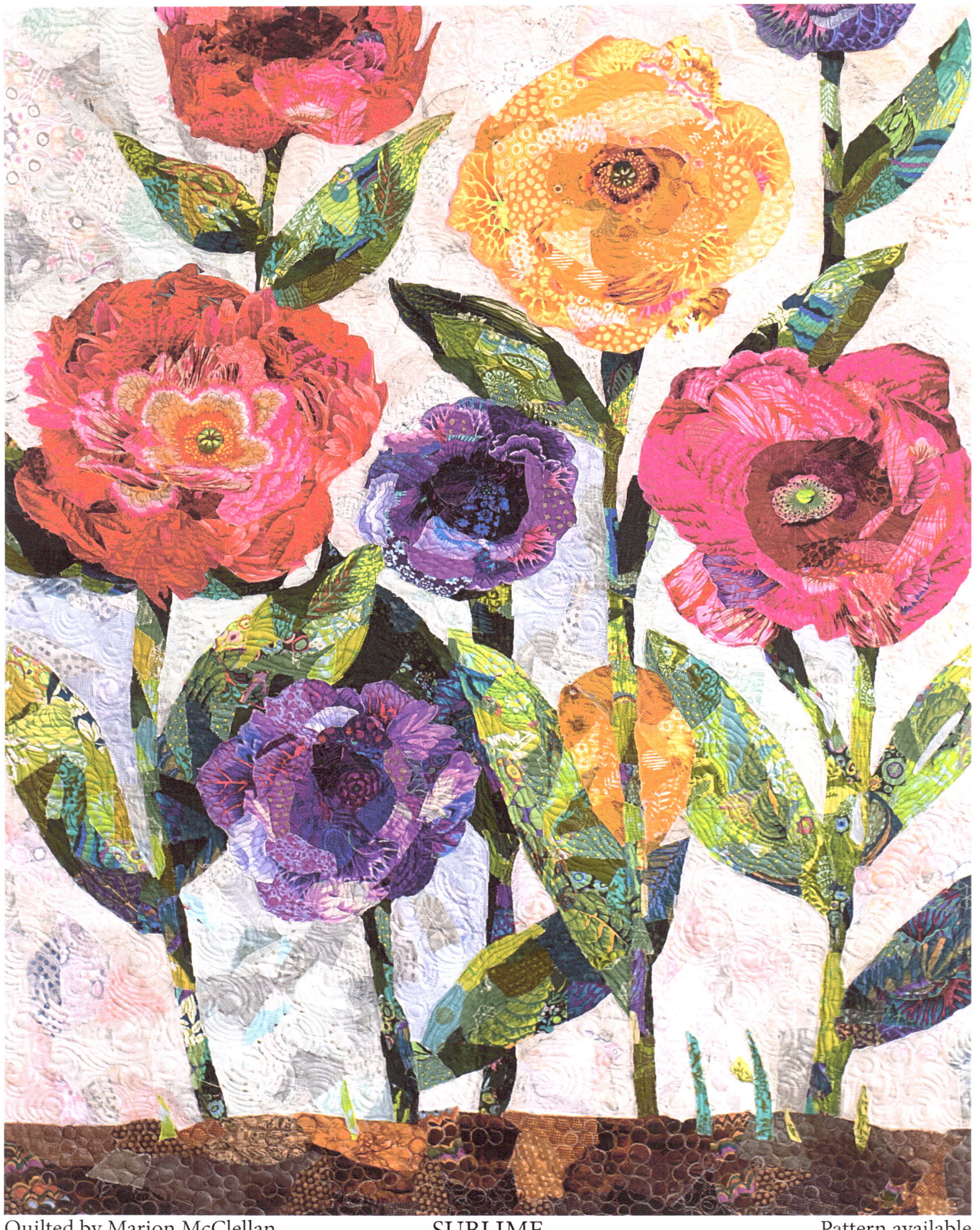

Quilted by Marion McClellan

SUBLIME
35" x 44"

Pattern available

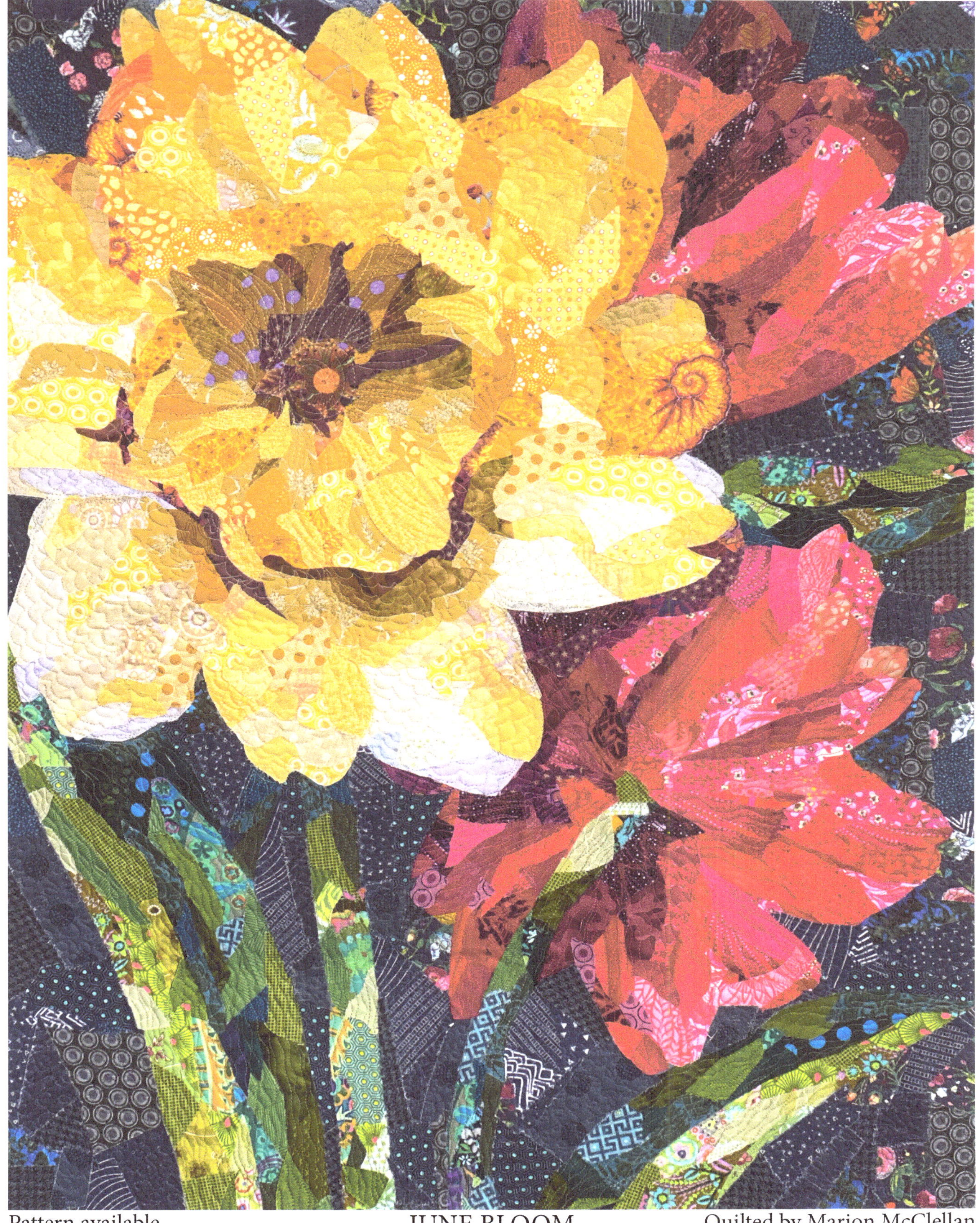

Pattern available

JUNE BLOOM
23" x 32"

Quilted by Marion McClellan

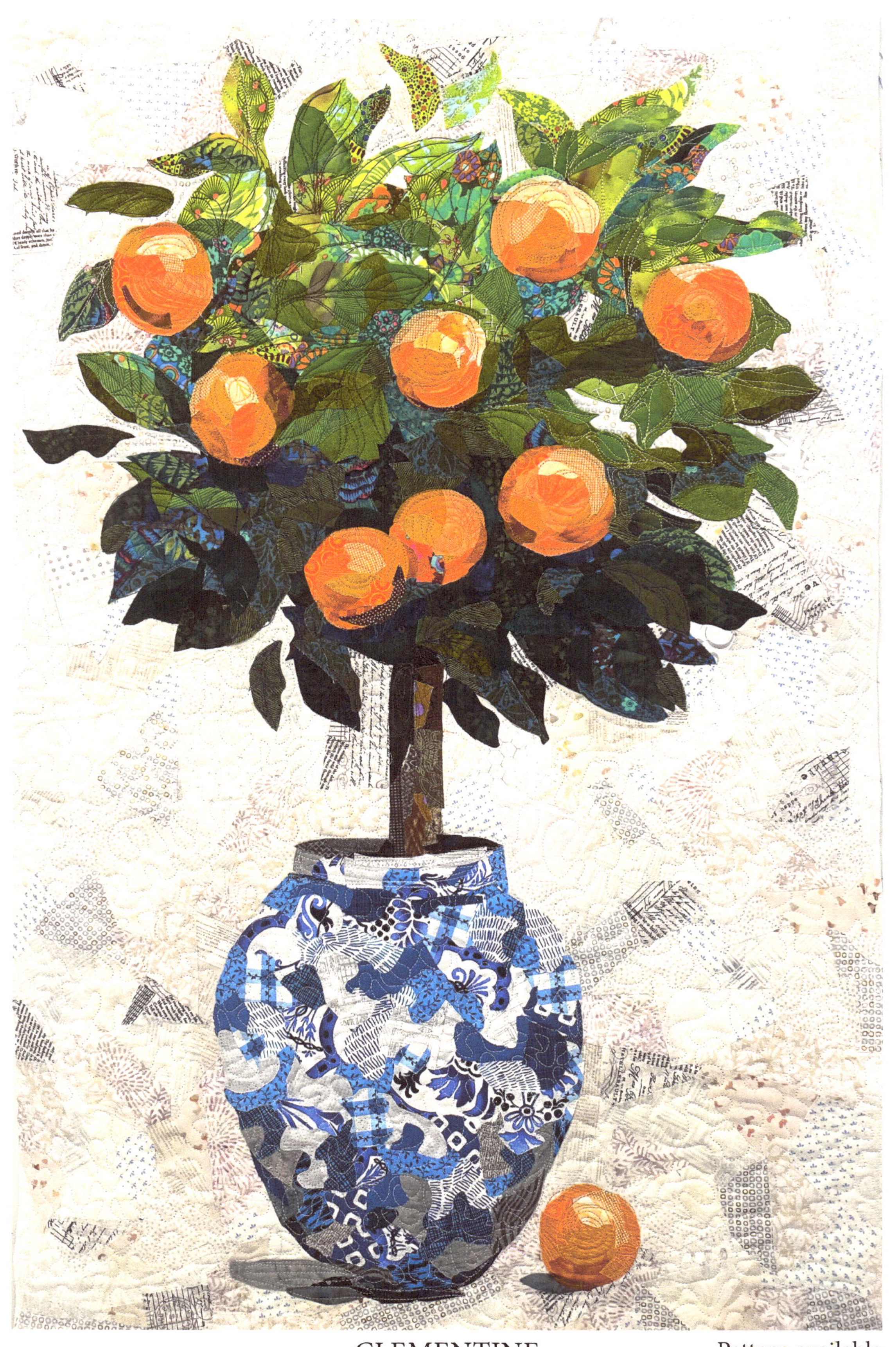

CLEMENTINE
24" x 36"

Pattern available

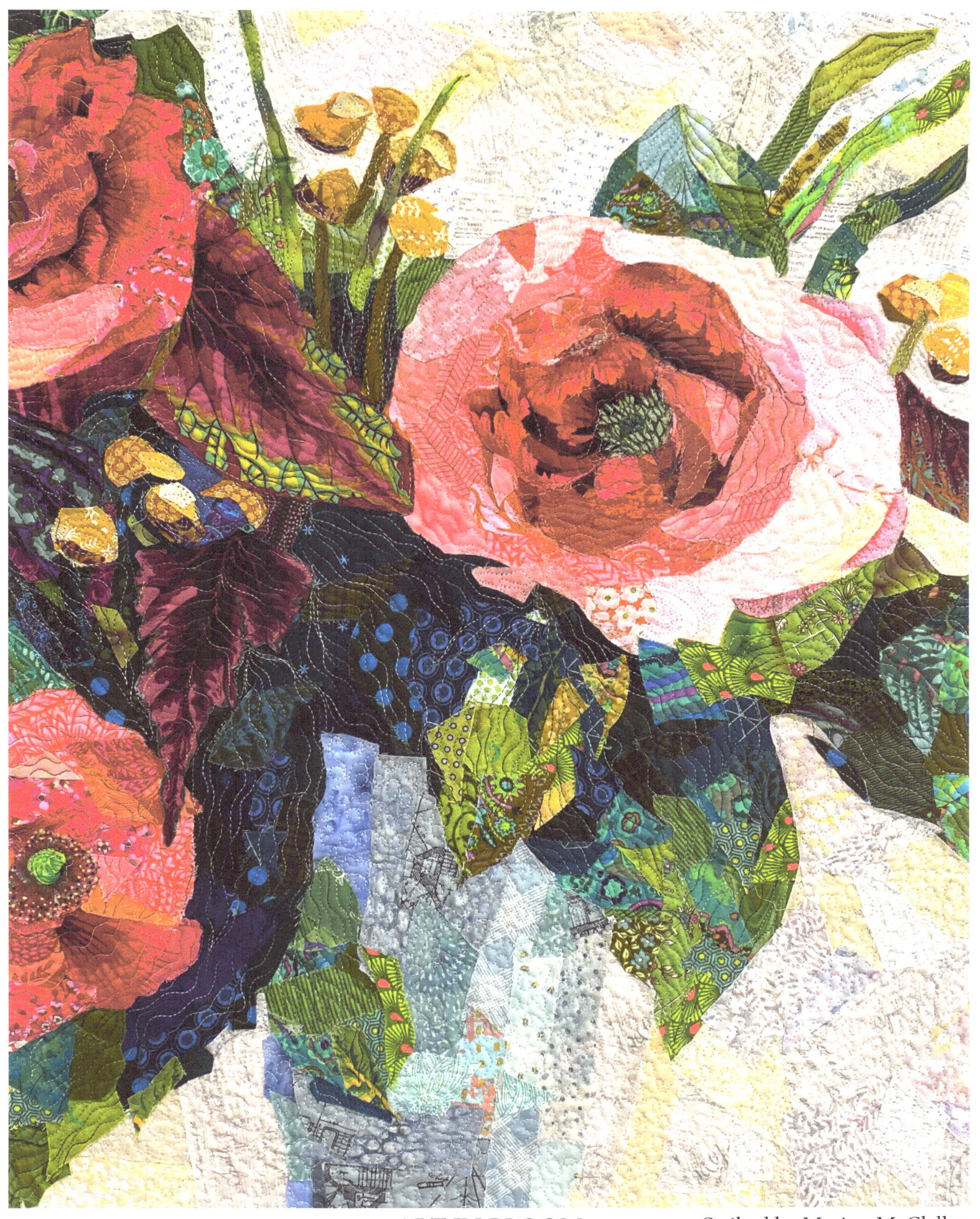

ART IN BLOOM
23" x 23"

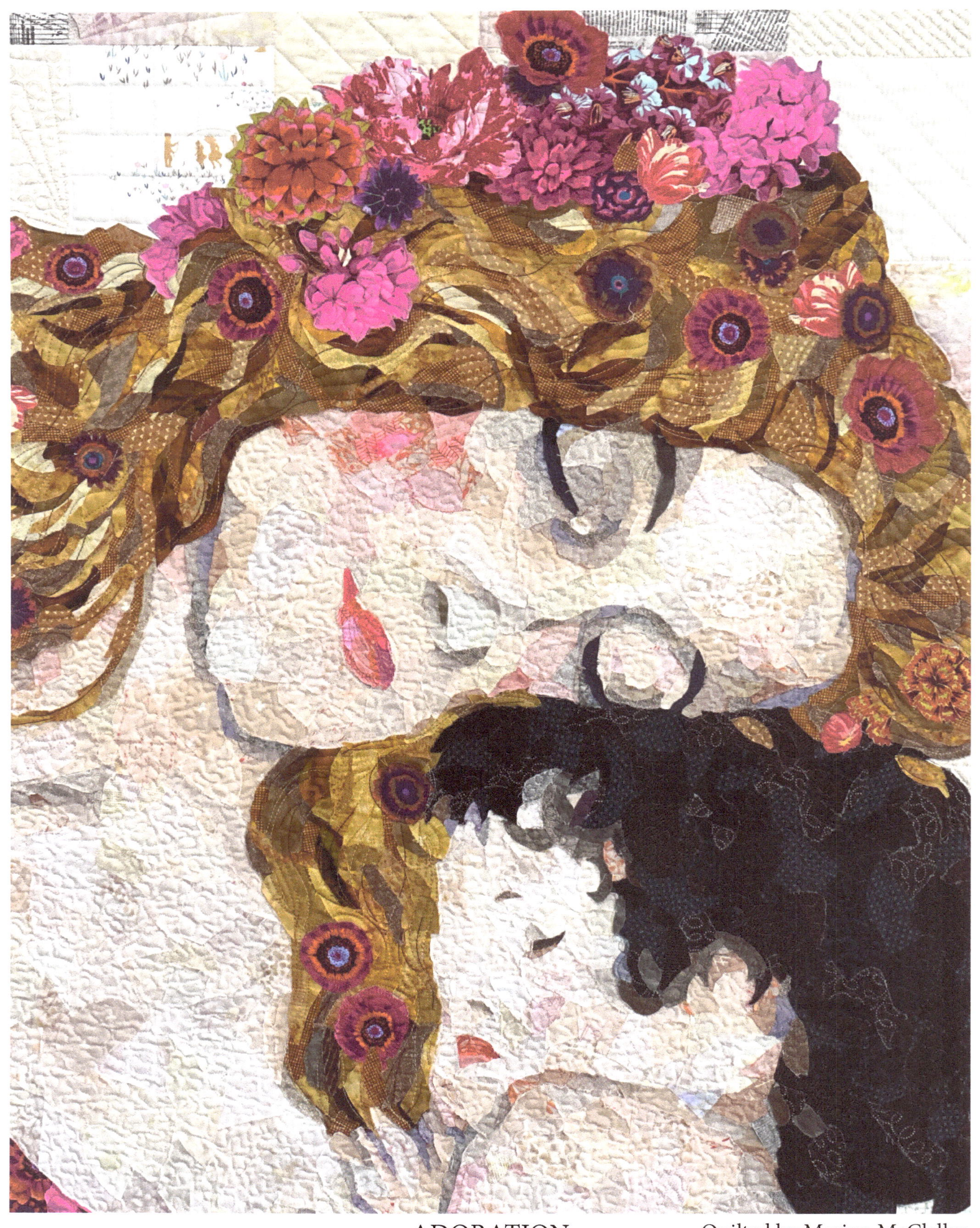

ADORATION

Quilted by Marion McClellan

40" x 52"

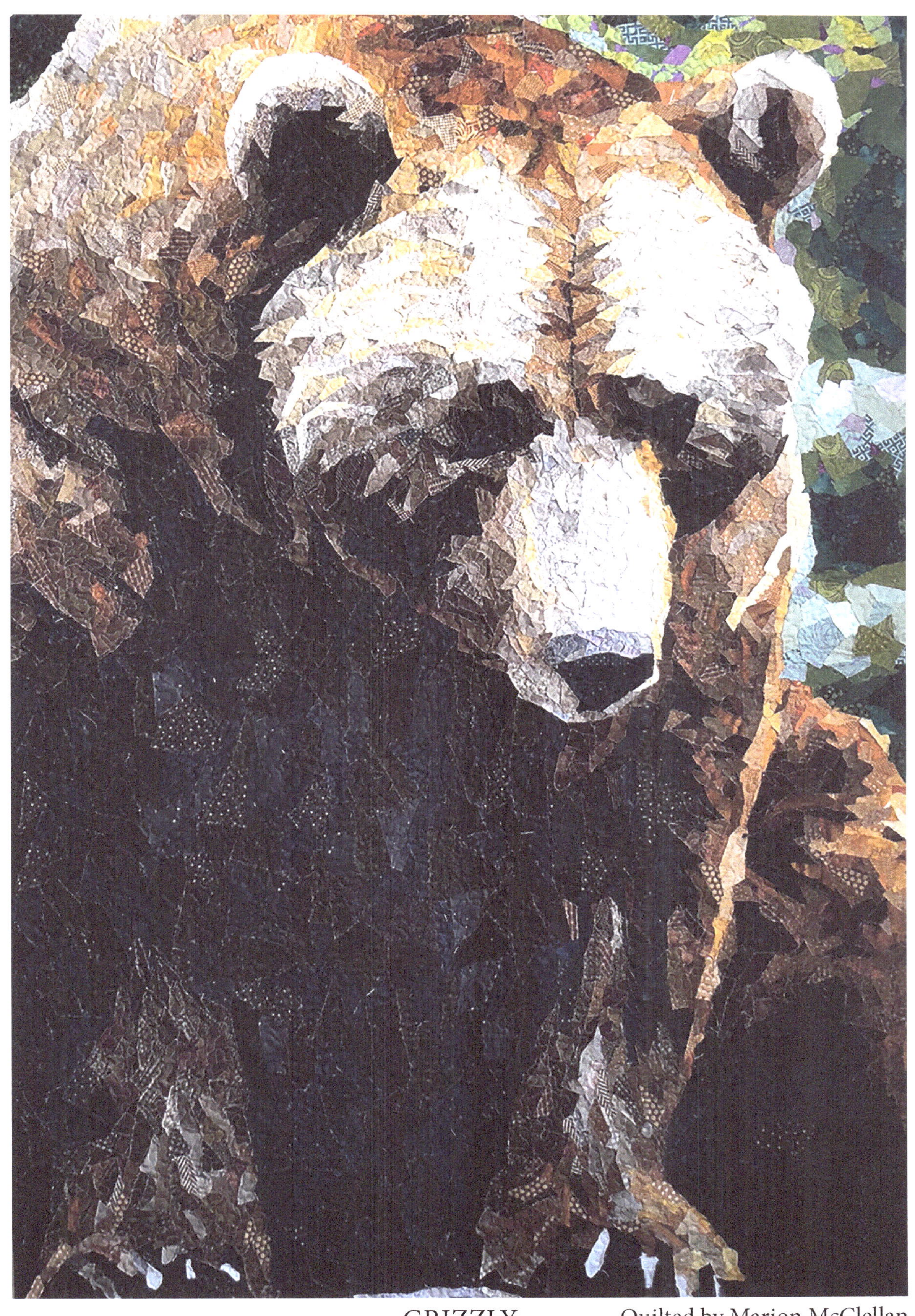

GRIZZLY
34" x 50"

Quilted by Marion McClellan

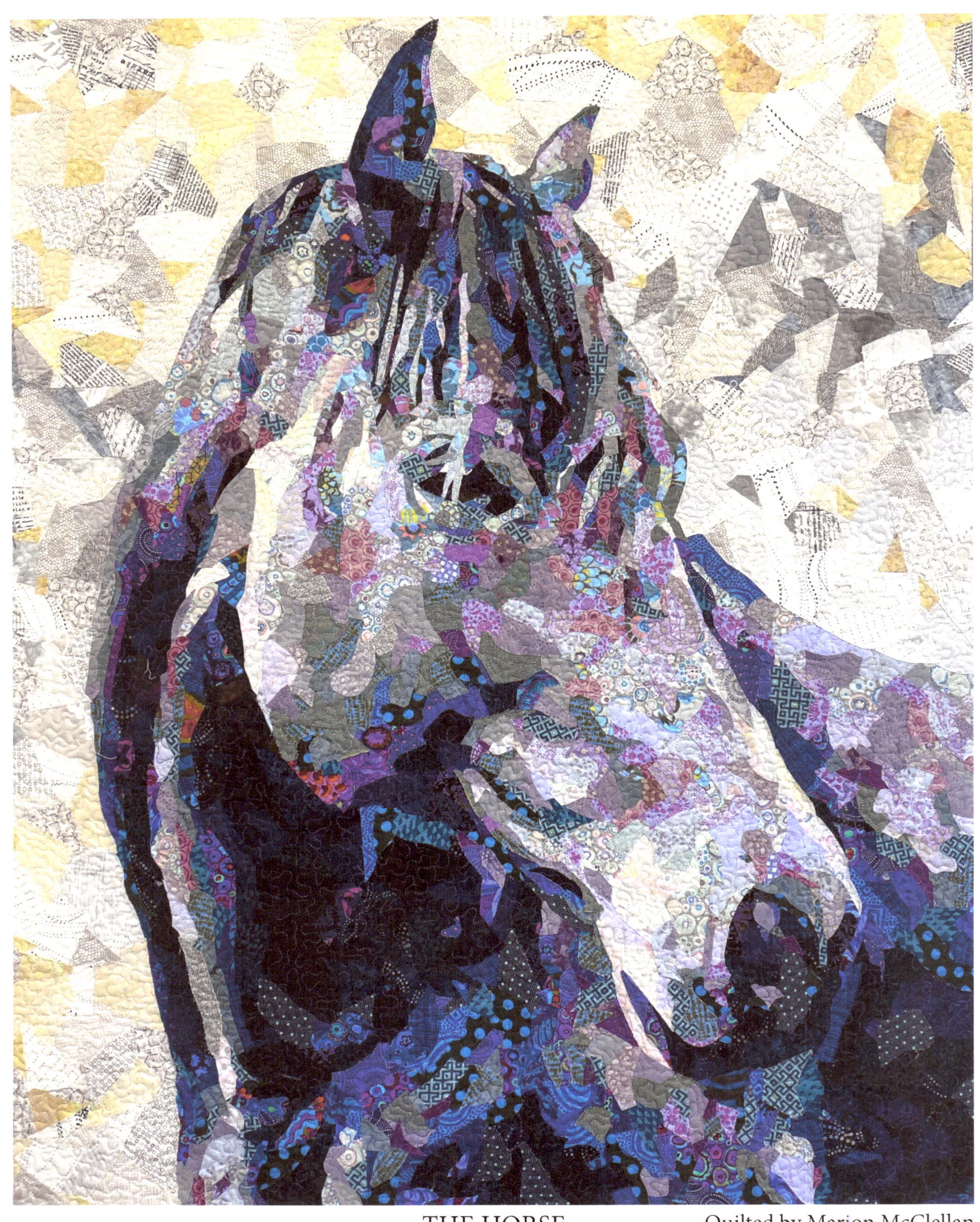

THE HORSE
36" x 50"

Quilted by Marion McClellan

Appendix

If you'd prefer to download PDFs of the full size bird templates, scan this QR code:

Full Size of Each Bird

Crane 11" x 33"

Duck 8" x 15"

Owl 11" x 18"

Quail 12" x 10"

Raven 13" x 13"

Swallow 8" x 11"

(Please note that discrepancies with printer settings may
slightly alter the final output size)

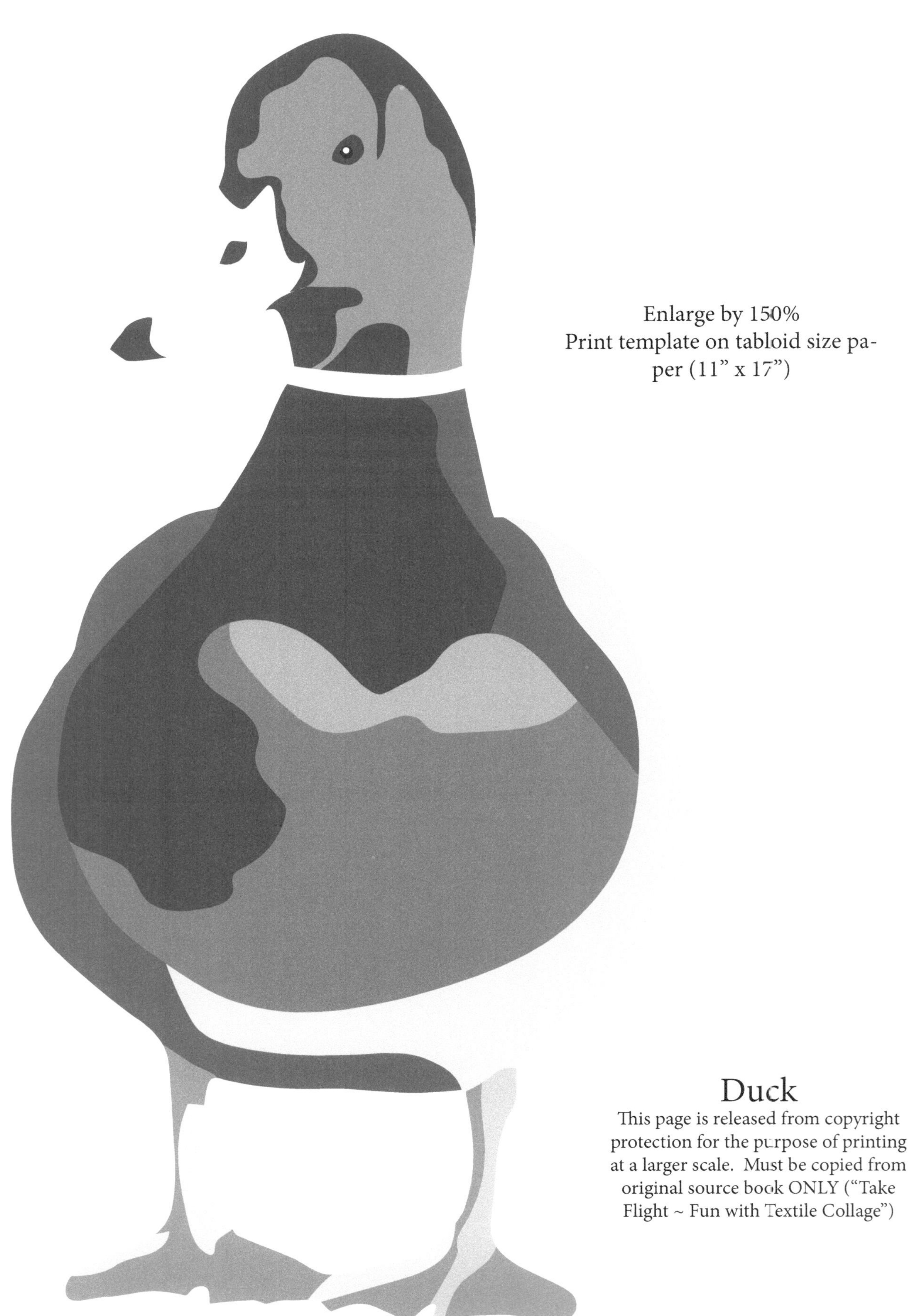

Duck

This page is released from copyright
protection for the purpose of printing
at a larger scale. Must be copied from
original source book ONLY ("Take
Flight ~ Fun with Textile Collage")

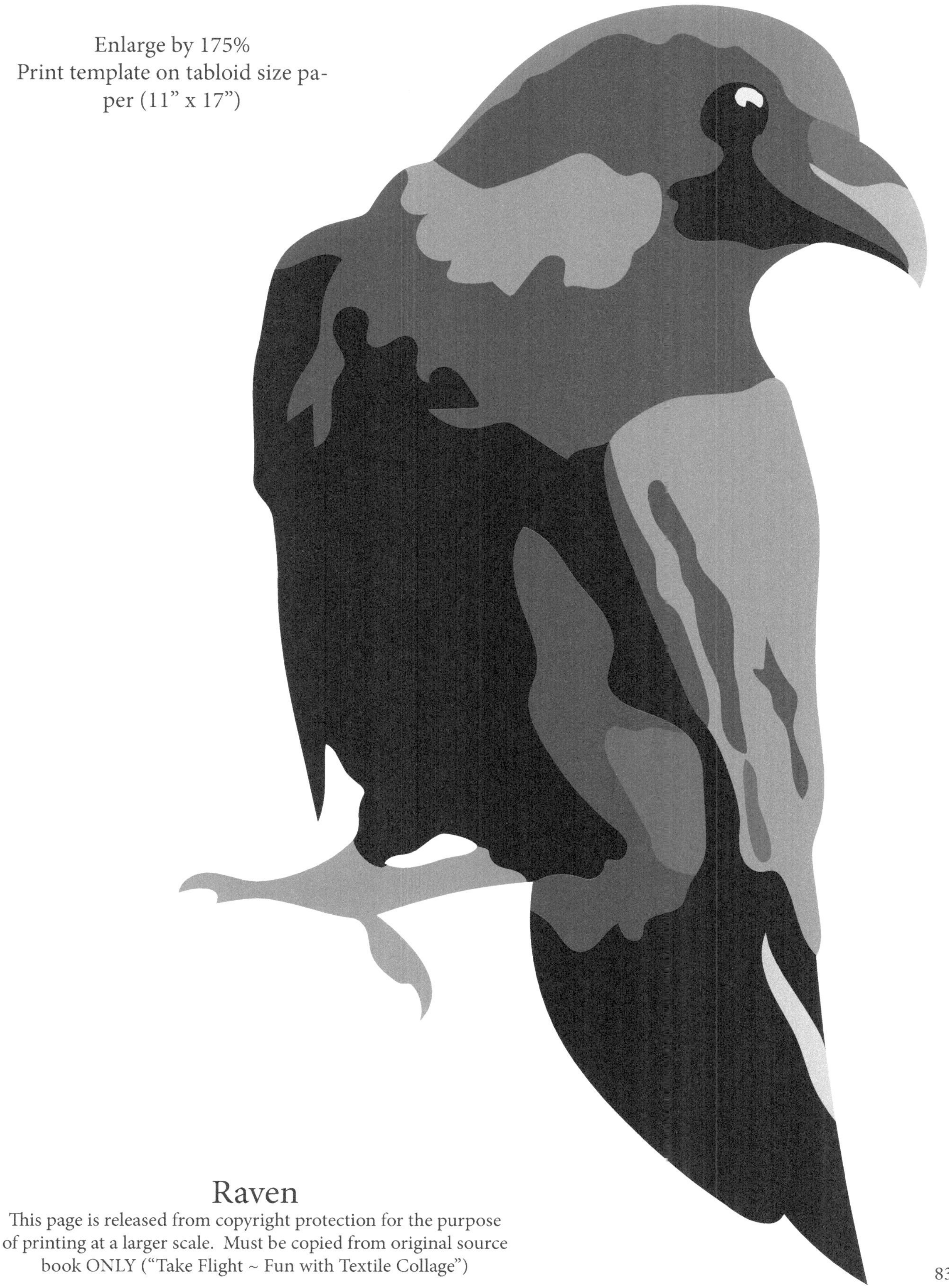

Raven

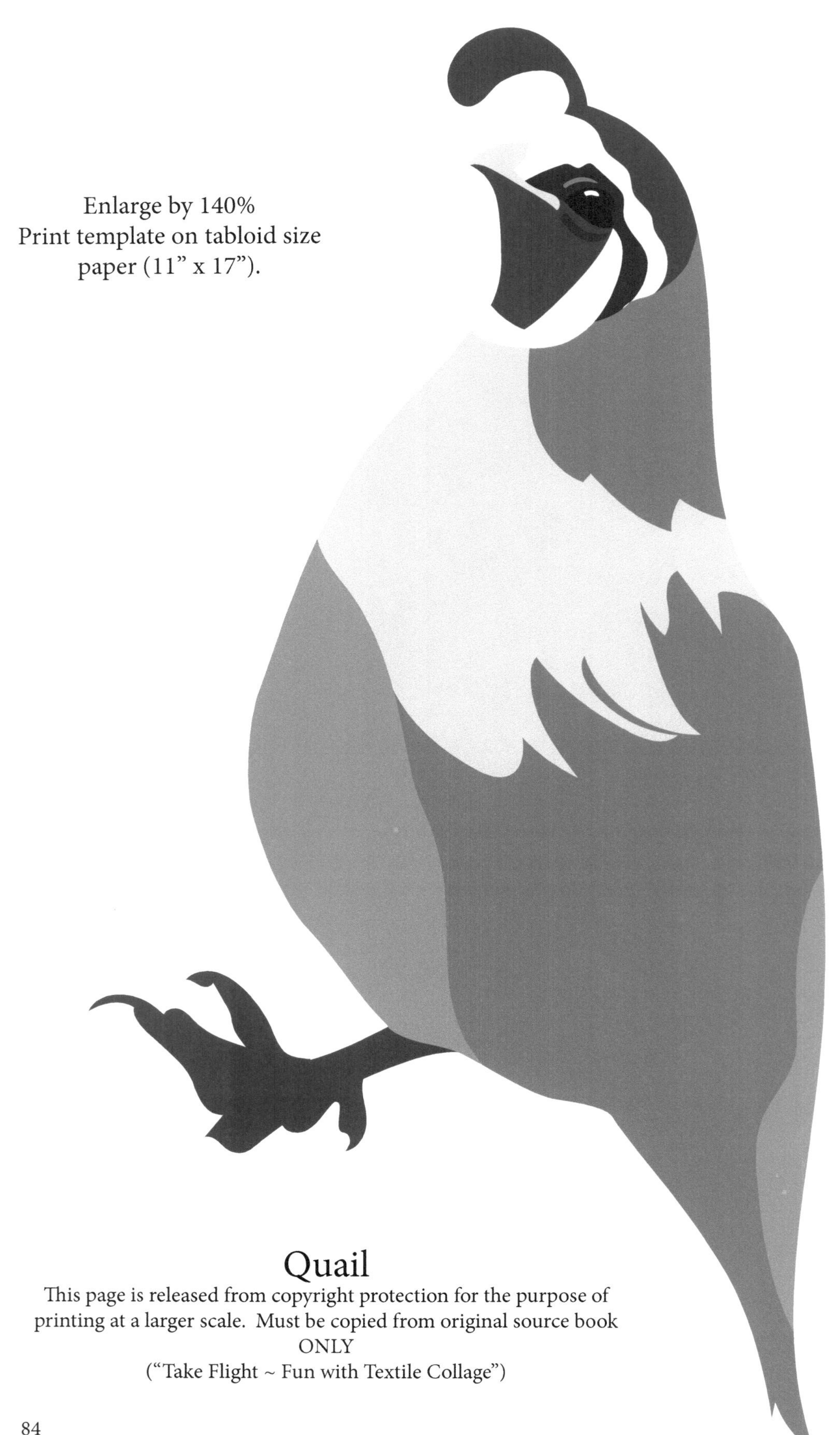

Quail

Crane

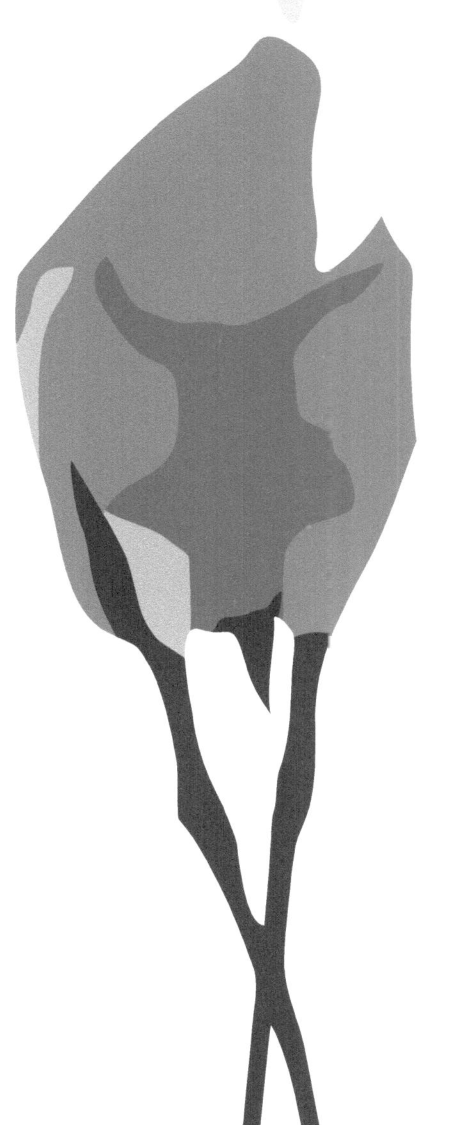

Enlarge by 1050%
Print template on 24" x 36" paper.

Enlarge by 117%
Print template on tabloid size paper
(11" x 17").

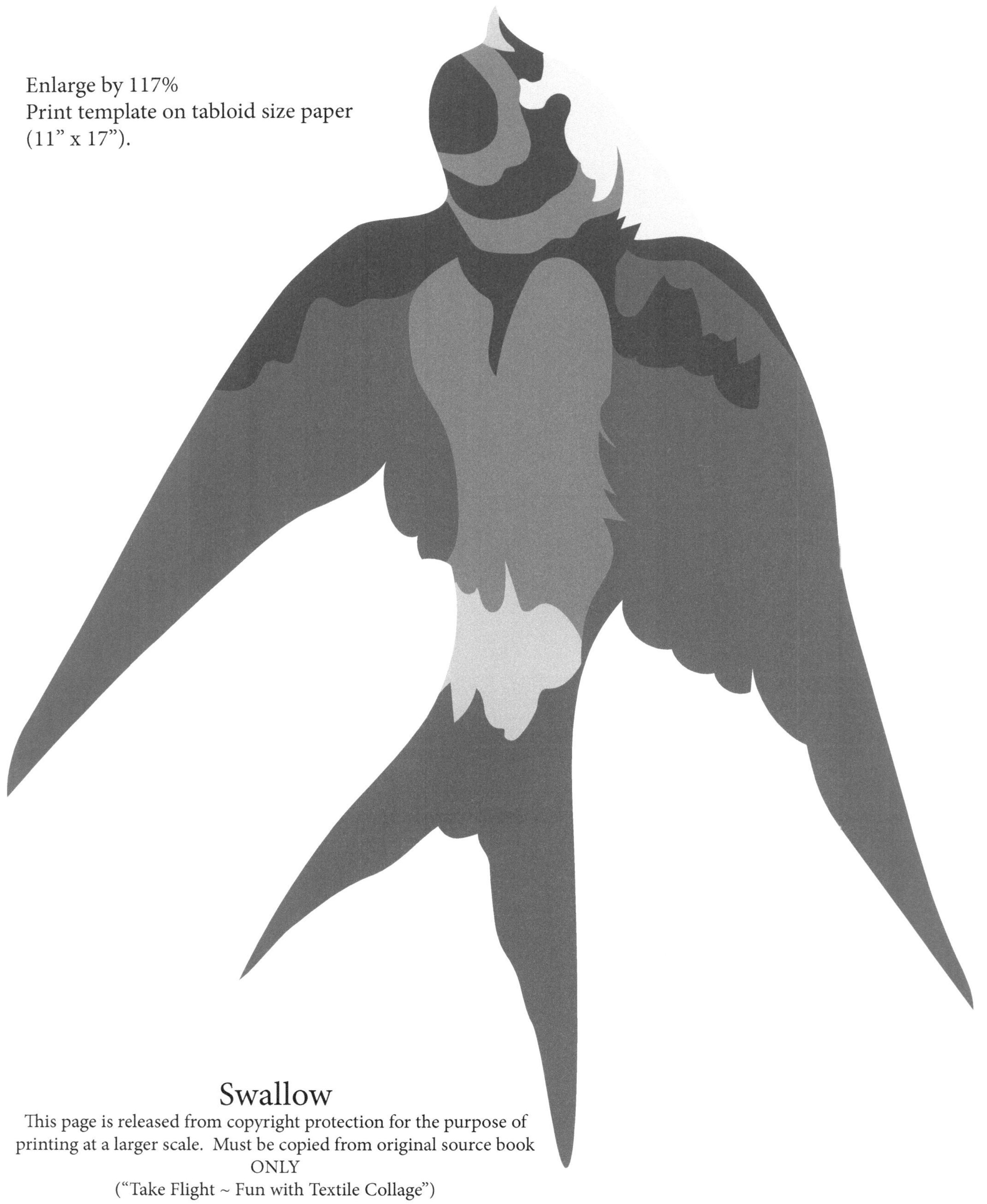

Swallow

This page is released from copyright protection for the purpose of
printing at a larger scale. Must be copied from original source book
ONLY
("Take Flight ~ Fun with Textile Collage")

86

Owl

This page is released from copyright protection for the purpose of printing at a larger scale. Must be copied from original source book ONLY ("Take Flight ~ Fun with Textile Collage")

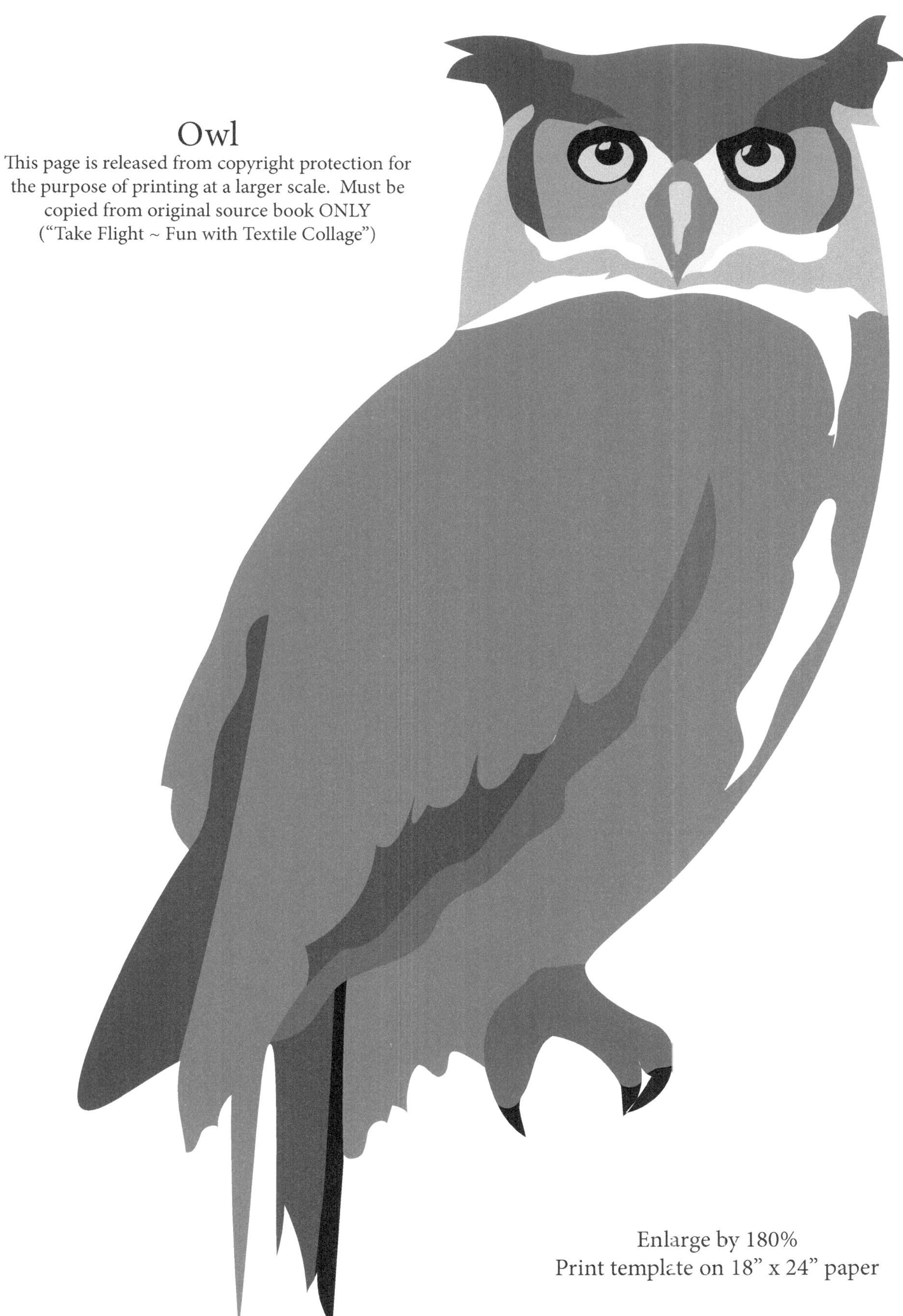

Enlarge by 180%
Print template on 18" x 24" paper

Complementary Elements

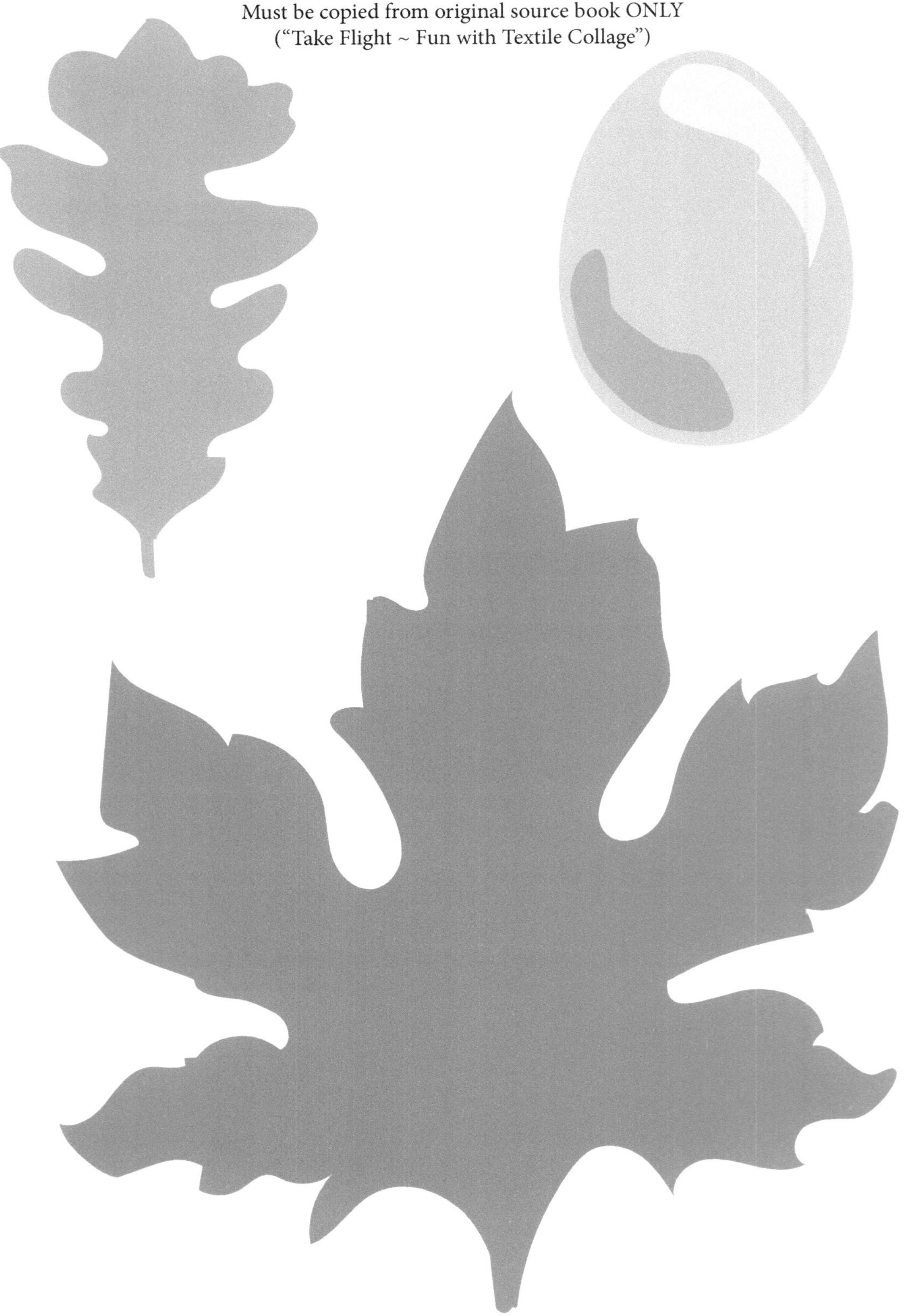

Use at 100%, no need to enlarge

Complementary Elements

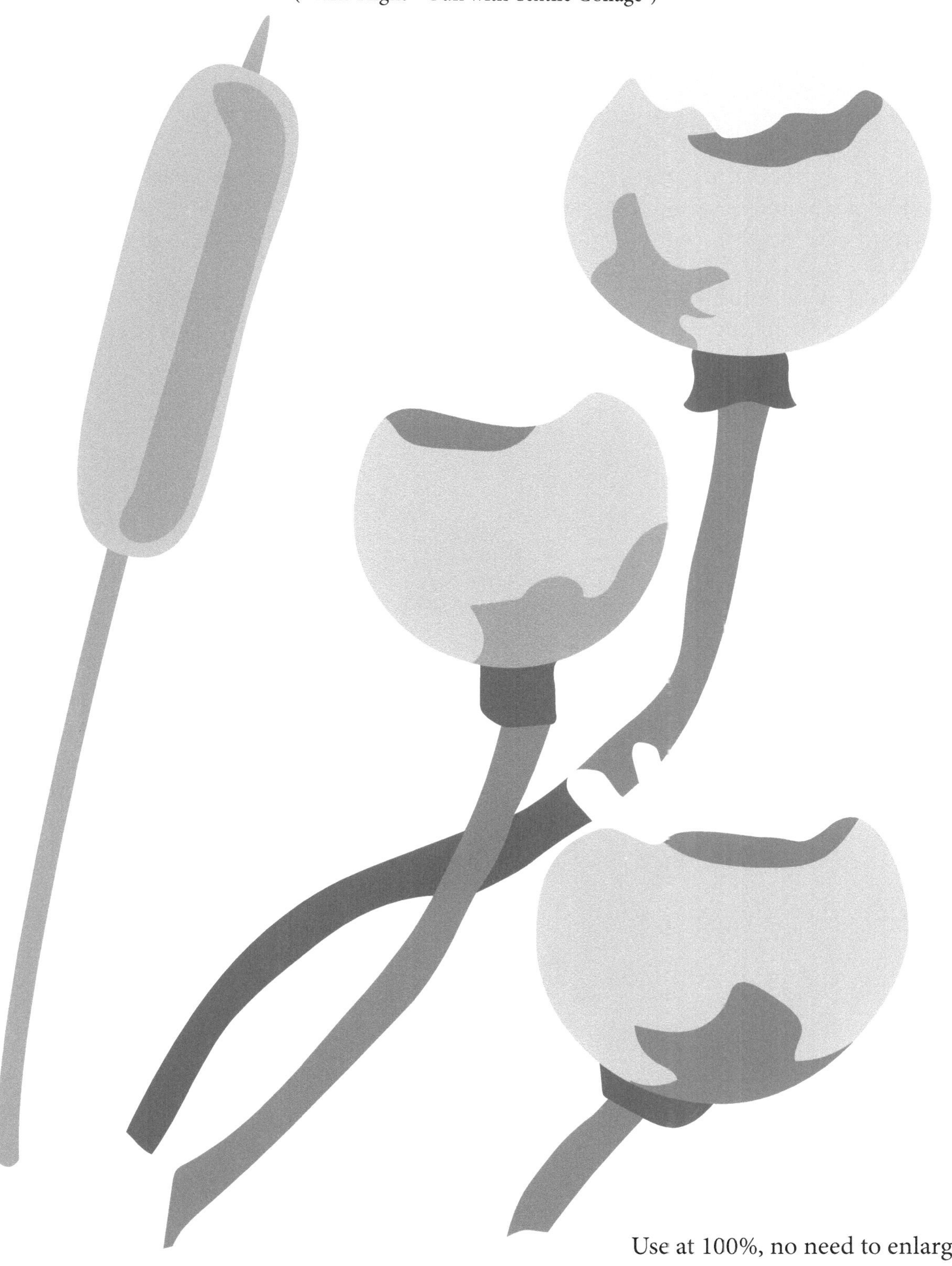

Use at 100%, no need to enlarge

About the Author

Emily Taylor is a self-taught artist, fabric designer and quilter. She has been a creative entrepreneur in both the home decor industry and quilt industry for 20+ years. Emily has been featured on QVC for her wallpaper murals and has created over a dozen fabric collections. Her foolproof collage quilt patterns combined with enthusiasm for teaching her students the secrets of success have generated a loyal following around the world.

Emily is the author of *Collage Quilter: Essentials for Success with Collage Quilts,* published in 2019. Her quilts have been featured in the quilt & craft magazines, *Art Quilting Studio, Be Creative,* and *Where Women Create.* She has also contributed to "The Quilt Show" television series.

Emily is an avid outdoor thrill seeker and loves to ski, mountain bike and hike with her husband and three children near their home in Sandy, Utah.

See more of Emily's work or contact her at
CollageQuilter.com

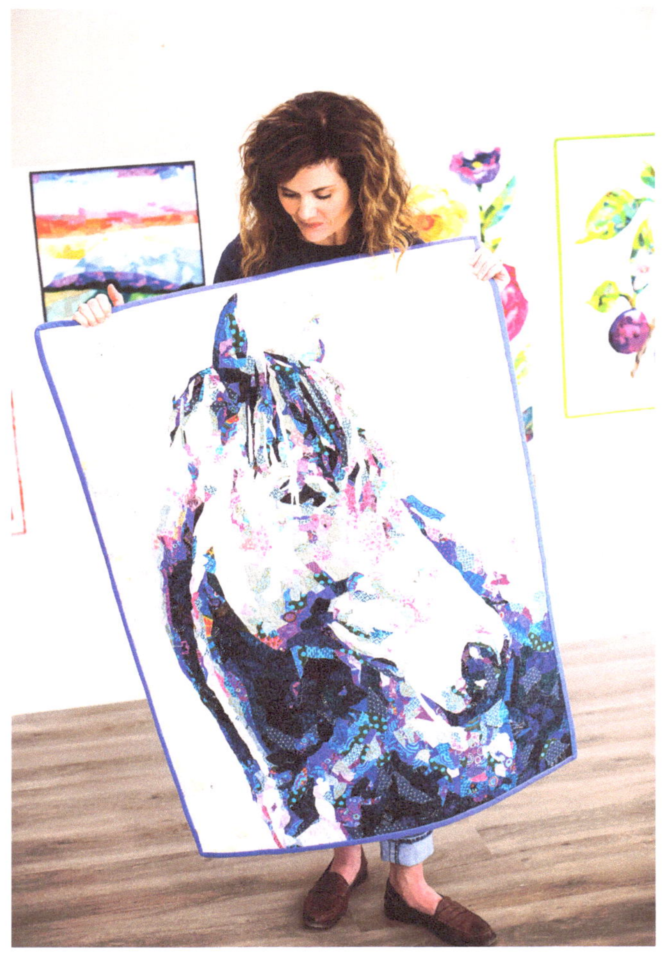

Additional Resources

Scan the QR codes by using your phone camera! They will link directly to the indicated web pages.

CollageQuilter.com
Patterns, Fabric, Supplies, Tutorials

Collage Quilter Academy
Comprehensive Video Tutorials

Collage.Quilter on Instagram
Behind the scenes and projects to inspire

Collage Quilter Academy Facebook Group
Tutorials, live video events and an engaged community working on group projects